Fred

PORTRAIT OF A FAST BOWLER

By the same author

VINTAGE SUMMER : 1947

The Cocked Trigger

Fred

PORTRAIT OF A FAST BOWLER

John Arlott

EYRE METHUEN
LONDON

First published 1971
© *1971 John Arlott*
Reprinted 1971, 1972 (three times) and 1973
Printed in Great Britain
for Eyre Methuen Ltd
11 New Fetter Lane, London EC4
by Whitstable Litho, Straker Brothers Ltd

SBN 413 27560 4

Contents

Illustrations

Plates

Acknowledgements and thanks for permission to reproduce the plates is due to Sport &
General Press Agency Ltd. for plates 1, 4, 6 and 11; A. Wilkes & Son for plate 2; The
Press Association for plate 3; Central Press Photos Ltd. for plates 5, 7, 8, 9 & 10.

Fred

PORTRAIT OF A FAST BOWLER

The Faces of Fred

The life of Fred Trueman is not a single story nor a simple pattern. There is not one Fred Trueman but four – the basic Fred Trueman, Fred Trueman the fast bowler, Fred Trueman the man, and Fred Trueman the public image. He is no one of these four: he is all four of them; and it is difficult to set any order or priority among them. The original Fred Trueman – the miner and son of a miner who, in 1949, set off from Maltby with wonder and hope to play cricket for Yorkshire – still exists, though he is more deeply buried than the usual youthful self that is contained within every man.

Fred Trueman the mature fast bowler was a sharply pointed and astutely directed weapon; Fred Trueman the man has often been tactless, haphazard, crude, a creature of impulse. In Fred Trueman the public image, so many accretions of rumour and fiction have been deposited round the human core that the resultant figure is recognizable only to those who do not know him. The four are not easily reconciled; but they exist within one body – or at least under the roof of one name – and to untwine them is to destroy the essential unity of a composite – but real – character. Of course many of the stories about Fred Trueman are apocryphal; many are not; but even those referring to situations that never existed are ingredients of him, for he is partly a myth – indeed, he accepted a place in mythology with some eagerness. His life is recorded in gossip as well as in *Wisden*.

The lad of eighteen who, after Ron Aspinall was injured,

played in four Championship matches of 1949 for Yorkshire would not arouse particular interest now; certainly he would not have done so in the middle nineteen-fifties: but 1949 was different. He was not remarkable but he was the uncomplicated, original Fred Trueman. He could not dream that he had come upon his historic cue. All cricketing England was as desperate for a fast bowler to fling back the humiliation imposed by Lindwall and Miller as ever America was for a white hope to humble Jack Johnson. By 1952 that hope had settled upon Fred Trueman and, if the primary Yorkshire character was not destroyed, it was soon encased in a new outer shell of what people wanted to see. He himself was to add fresh layers of behaviour which completed the Trueman of the public image. Even the final picture is not to be defined. A reigning Prime Minister – Harold Wilson, himself a Huddersfield man – described him as 'the greatest living Yorkshireman': while Roy Ullyett made him the subject of his most violently funny caricature (see page 143).

He played cricket for twenty years at first-class level – until the late nineteen-sixties, when he was thirty-seven, far past the fast-bowler's normal allotted span, which ends at thirty – and he took more wickets in Test cricket than anyone else has ever done. In that time the bounding energy and fierce pace of youth matured to a semi-instinctive, but also extremely shrewd, technique in handling the fast bowling machine that was a body perfectly constructed for precisely that purpose. For a decade – again much longer than the peak period of even the best of the kind – he was, when the fire burnt, as fine a fast bowler as any.

All this time he was travelling the world, acquiring experience, but still capable of quite boyish brashness; a creature of impulse and emotion who, almost beyond his own control, acquired a reputation – often, but not always, deserved – for violence and four-letter words.

At length that reputation slopped over. There is a histrionic

streak in him and, if the men of his own county insisted on
seeing him as the archetypal Yorkshireman they themselves
wanted to be – blunt, honest, strong, destroying bowler of high
speed, smiter of sixes, taker of acrobatic catches, striker of wise-
cracks, cocker of snooks at authority – he was only too happy –
in fact compulsively eager – to play the part. A newspaper
column in which, freed from the former control of the Yorkshire cricket authorities, he can state strong opinions; a year
round the North country clubs with a vaudeville act which
the modest – and some not so modest – found 'blue', have deep-
ened the artificial layers about the original Fred Trueman. Yet,
peel it away and, at every level, you have Fred Trueman in
varying degrees of his four personalities.

Those four identities, too, are often completely contradictory.
He can be uproarious but also – though not often – silent,
moody; he can be generous – and mean; he could bowl his
heart out – or turn it in; he can be harsh – or gentle; he can be
genuinely witty – and horribly crude; almost hysterically funny
– and a complete bore; he can be intuitively understanding –
and chillingly embarrassing: he can be arrogant – and as uncertain of himself as a schoolboy; he is pulled this way and that
by his doubts and his emotions; he wants desperately to be
liked and he is, at bottom, lonely. Least of all is it generally
understood that, in the urge to succeed at the craft in which he
excelled, he lived constantly on the sharpest edge of his nerves.

No one can be sure of holding a true balance between all the
constituents of this man of conflicting characters. Indeed, no
man can accurately describe another; he cannot even know
him because he cannot discover all, while the other, however
willing he might be, is not capable of letting anyone else know
all about him. No one knows Fred Trueman completely; and
none of those who know him at all would agree about him –
if only for the fact that no two of them have seen the same
Fred Trueman.

The unifying thread running through all the apparent contraditions is that of the fast bowler; not simply a man who bowled fast, nor a man who became a fast bowler, but one who knew from the first moment he considered such matters that he was going to be a great fast bowler. Others of expert knowledge might doubt it: he never did. He realized that there had to be a period – while he grew up – before the rest of the world realized it: but that was the only qualification he allowed. He was not merely a fast bowler in achievement, he was a fast bowler in the mind and in the heart. There is no characteristic fast bowler. Although Trueman and Statham, Statham and Tyson were so effectively complementary, they were, and are, even more different in personality than in bowling method. Fred Trueman was the kind of fast bowler he had created for himself; a larger-than-life-sized figure compounded in the imagination of a boy from the fancies, facts, loyalties, cricket, reading, traditions and all the other influences of a semi-rural, semi-industrial area of South Yorkshire in the nineteen-thirties. Whenever he acted in a considered fashion – and he did not always do so at the most important junctures of his career – he acted as that ideal fast bowler who lived in his mind would have done.

This is an attempt to reflect those two fast bowlers in one, the outward and visible Fred and his inward and spirited aim: by one who has observed him and talked with him from the beginning of his cricket career to its end; who has admired him and blushed for him; felt sorry for him, and indignant on his behalf; thought him fortunate and unfortunate; sought him out, avoided him; relaxed with him, been anxious for him; been delighted by him, been bored by him; and, at the moments of his greatness as a bowler, been stirred by what he could do with a cricket ball.

It is an attempt to paint all four Truemans, warts and all – not only his own warts, but the warts other people have stuck on him – often without his knowledge.

Of course this is not a first-hand biography. No one could write a first-hand biography of Fred who has lived in a world where constantly someone or other said 'Have you heard the new one about Fred?' or 'Did you hear Fred's latest' or 'Do you know what so-and-so thinks about Fred?' In April 1968, in India to play in a Flood Relief Fund match, he was sitting in the lounge of a Bombay hotel one evening when his neighbour, the Australian batsman, Norman O'Neill, leant over and said, 'Fred, I believe those two Indians at the next table are talking about you.' The reply was instant and unaffected, 'Ay, they talk about me all over t'world, Norm, lad'.

CHAPTER TWO

Father of the Man

Scotch Springs is such a place as the Industrial Revolution and accidents of geology combine to scatter about the North of England. It is a terrace of twelve brick-built houses, each closely-set pair of front doors capped by a gabled porch. From their backs rich, dark ploughland runs to the village of Stainton, something over half a mile north-west. On the other side of the terrace, above the pocket of coal set in the farmland, is the vast grey whaleback, wrinkled with rain runnels, of the tip; the gaunt shaft and all the harsh surface works of Maltby Main, one of the most important mines in the south Yorkshire coalfield.

Fred Trueman, the fourth of Alan Thomas Trueman's seven children, was born at number five Scotch Springs on 6 February, 1931. The extravagance of the Trueman legend may be said to have begun at birth, when his weight was 14 lbs 1 oz. No record survives of any comment. He was christened Frederick Sewards – the latter his grandmother's surname – in Stainton Church.

By January 1971 the coal tip had pressed up on Scotch Springs: number five, like half the other houses in the row, was derelict, its windows broken and doors boarded. 'The colliery wants the land,' said one of the women who remained. When this appears in print the last of Scotch Springs will be buried under the waste of the pit.

Trueman senior, the son of a stud groom, was one of many grateful to find work in the pits during the slump of the early thirties, and he worked at the coal face in Maltby Main. A keen and useful left-arm bowler and batsman in local club cricket, he taught all his sons the game and encouraged them to play. Fred Trueman spent much spare time of his childhood in Stainton, a typically English village of two or three hundred people, where he went to his first school. It is now being 'in-filled', to use the planners' term, with ambitious residential development between the cottages.

There was plenty of cricket and regular evening practice on the pleasant small ground at Stainton until, when Fred was twelve, the family moved to Maltby on the other side of the colliery. Tennyson Road, Maltby is newer than Scotch Springs and number ten – red brick and tile, just across the road from a well-trodden football ground – is larger than the earlier house. It is part of the concentrated housing within walking distance of the colliery where virtually all the employed males of the district work; and near the centre – a cross roads, the largest pub, called the Queens, the Grand Cinema (also Bingo), a working men's club and some shops – of a town of some 10,000 population. It is a two-storey town, apart from a few ambitious gestures like Millards emporium; and its size and atmosphere are such that everyone knows, or knows about, everyone else; and no one is so far out of the swim as not to know Fred Trueman and to recall clearly some dramatic incident – true or untrue, but firmly believed – of his early life.

The switch from the village school at Stainton to Maltby Modern offered more opportunities for cricket, organized there by two masters, Mr Stubbs and Mr Harrison, who encouraged the young Trueman's ambition to be a fast bowler. He played for the school at football and rugby, too, and in the classroom laid the foundations of quick reading and retentive memory through which he is more deeply versed in cricket history and statistics than many first-class players who had more pretentious educations.

Playing for the school at Wickersley, near Rotherham – and

batting, like many a boy before and since without a protector
– he was hit in the groin by a fastish bowler. He was taken to
hospital in Sheffield for emergency treatment and for nearly
two years – significantly for him two complete cricket seasons –
he was virtually immobilised, and under treatment for an injury
so serious that at one point dire consequences were feared.
Through that depressing period, Messrs Stubbs and Harrison,
with admirable sympathy, sustained his enthusiasm for cricket
by arranging for him to score or umpire in school matches until,
at fourteen and a half, he left to work in the local newsagent's
shop.

If at this point he had been less than wholly committed, not
merely to cricket but to becoming a fast bowler, the injury and
consequent inhibitions, loss of practice and progress must have
caused him to give up the game. His conviction, though, was
complete; so complete that it carried along with him not only
his father, who was predisposed to sympathise, but his brothers,
sisters and mother as well. He joined a club called Roche Abbey
and in his first four matches took twenty-five wickets at a total
cost of thirty-seven runs.

This helped him to bridge the gap – not so wide in Yorkshire
as in other parts of England, but still a fact even there –
between boys' and men's cricket. His few matches for Roche
Abbey brought him an invitation to go on a southern tour with
a Yorkshire Federation boys' team that included Brian Close.
This was an advance, but he remained impatient. He was now
working in the pit as a haulage hand with the tubs, and this
helped to harden him physically: but both he and his father
realised that if he was to continue to make progress he needed
to play in better cricket than he could find in Maltby. Sheffield
was the obvious centre for him: he applied to join the Sheffield
United club, at the beginning of the 1948 season, only to find
the membership closed. Elsewhere this might have proved a
long term, if not an insuperable check: but the Yorkshire
system worked, as it usually does.

Sheffield has not played the important part in the county's cricket since the first World War that it did in earlier days. In some directions that is no bad thing: it means that no good potential is likely to be overlooked, and there is always someone keen to renew the credit of the district by the production of an outstanding performer. Cyril Turner, a left-hand bat and right-arm medium bowler for Yorkshire between the two wars, became professional to the Sheffield United club after 1945. In response to a carefully argued letter from Trueman senior, he watched Fred bowling, recognised the spark of talent, and persuaded the committee to reopen its membership to let him in.

The youngster's purpose and the excellence of his action made an impression: but he was yet appreciably short of his full height: often when he strove for extra pace his delivery became a sling, and he lost both length and direction. After a few matches for the Sheffield Second XI, and some expert guidance by Cyril Turner on his grip and his follow-through, he was brought into the club's Yorkshire Council team for the last five matches of the season when he took fifteen wickets.

Once more the Yorkshire system proved itself. The seventeen-year-old was erratic and inexperienced; but he had a basically good delivery and the positive merit of speed. That information was transmitted to the county's cricket committee and during the winter he was summoned – expenses paid – to Leeds for the indoor winter coaching classes under Bill Bowes and Arthur – 'Ticker' – Mitchell.

They watched and studied him and were convinced that his delivery swing – which argued his case as a young player more effectively than anyone or anything else, and saved his county career – was so essentially fine that all else had to be built round it. The first need was for control. He had to learn to bowl within himself, to use only as much pace as allowed him to maintain accurate length and line. He tended to over-pitch; and, for years after he should have known better, his response to anything in a batsman which displeased him – an edged

stroke, a narrow escape, an effective stroke, above all, a successful hook – was the bouncer, dug in regardless of the state of the
pitch or the batsman's ability to hook. It was late in life that he
learned to threaten the bumper so convincingly that the batsman moved on to the back foot to deal with it, and then bowl
him out with a yorker. Control for him was primarily a matter
of temperament. In the nets he could maintain an accuracy
which seemed beyond him under the tension of actual play.

He dragged his right foot an inordinate distance, but it was
decided that any attempt to cure that fault might destroy
much that went before : although subsequent changes in the
laws were to make his drag a serious embarrassment, that
decision was certainly correct. Some detailed but crucial altera-
tions in the landing of his feet in the three strides of the actual
delivery involved changing physical acts that had become automatic, but they were tested and practised until they, in their
turn, were assimilated.

Bill Bowes has always said that Fred Trueman was the ideal
pupil, not only desperately anxious to learn, but unquestion-
ingly obedient and untiring in practice. So this was a winter of
improvement, though at the end of it the decision was still
'Superb action, fairly fast, but. . . .'

Yorkshire have no formal relations with their younger players,
whose enthusiasm has generally made it possible for the county
committee to be autocratic in its dealings with them. Their
telegram summoning the young fast bowler from Maltby to
play against Cambridge University on 11, 12 and 13 May, 1949,
meant simply what it said, but not what he and his family
inferred from it. He was single-mindedly ambitious about his
future in cricket; but when the county's invitation arrived –
indeed, when he took the field at Fenners – he had never played
for the Second XI, nor even seen a first-class match; and he
had next to no understanding of cricket politics.

The fact is that, when Yorkshire invited him to play at
Cambridge, he had no place in their future plans. For years

the county, to the pique of some of its opponents, has contrived
three or four 'friendly' matches – against MCC, the Universities and perhaps a touring side – as high quality practice before
they engage themselves fully in the graver business of the County
Championship. The scores of these 'non-business' matches in
Wisden, especially over a few years after the last War, contain
the names of sometimes a couple of players, generally pace
bowlers, who were virtually never heard of again. Yorkshire
conscientiously try out cricketers who have reached a certain
standard in their nets or in serious – preferably Yorkshire
Council – club cricket. These early matches are constantly used
to eliminate borderline players.

The new bowler they took to Cambridge could well have
been intended for elimination – like six other opening bowlers
who appeared in Yorkshire's University fixtures of the next five
years. It was all but impossible to see a place for him within
the county's current strategy: in respect of pace bowlers they
were already, to use a Yorkshire expression, 'suited'.

At the level of first principles, Yorkshire are the last of the
counties to be impressed by sheer pace. As historic fact they
have had few truly fast bowlers, because they have always made
accuracy their first demand and, hence, have generally preferred
the medium or fast-medium bowler with his capacity for control, economy and long spells, rather than thè man of higher
speed who is likely to be less precise, less flexible in technique
and capable of fewer overs. At this time their opening bowlers,
both fast-medium, were already established: Alec Coxon – who
had played for England against Australia in the previous year
– and Ron Aspinall, a strong young man of high promise who
had made good his place in 1948. They had both loosened their
arms in the two preceding matches, against the New Zealanders
and the Championship fixture with Somerset and now, since
they were likely to have a heavy summer, they were being rested:
hence the vacancy for Trueman. Norman Yardley was a capable
third seam bowler in a team which would always maintain the

traditional balance with at least two spin bowlers. Brian Close, the strongly fancied new all-rounder, could bowl both medium paced outswing and off-spin: he would be the other opening bowler at Fenners. All this was sufficient to remove any need for a new pace bowler. If one should be wanted in the future, Yorkshire already had two actively in mind. Bill Foord, now qualified as a school teacher, and John Whitehead, an undergraduate at London University, had been prevented by their studies from playing regularly: but Whitehead since 1946 and Foord from a year later, had turned out in occasional matches for the county after the end of the summer term. Both in their early twenties and experienced club cricketers, they had attracted interest beyond Yorkshire for pace above medium to an extent impressive in English cricket of the immediate post-war years. Neither was available in mid-May; but the need was not yet urgent. Other young pace bowlers, too, were in mind, such as Brooke, McHugh, George Padgett and Barraclough: but they had all been seen in Second XI or Council matches in the Leeds area. There was too, an awareness of local interests; justice to Sheffield must be seen to be done in Sheffield.

Yorkshire alone among the first-class counties do not maintain a ground staff. Traditionally a Yorkshire cap is hard to win; harder than an England cap, they say in Yorkshire; and certainly Yorkshiremen have played for their country before they were capped by their county. Thus, while contracted young players competing for established places in other counties know one another from regular contact on the ground staff, those of Yorkshire often do not. The rival is also a stranger and usually the more keenly resented for that fact. Competition for caps can be harsh and, even in the case of players of outstanding potential, long drawn-out. Len Hutton fought for his place as opening batsman with Ken Davidson (who subsequently made a high reputation as a badminton player). Bill Bowes disputed his cap with Frank Dennis, later Len Hutton's brother-in-law; Johnnie Wardle was matched with Alan Mason for the place of slow left arm bowler; and in 1970 Neil Smith and David Bairstow competed for the wicket-keeper's place left by the retirement of Jimmy Binks.

The objective captain or county selector can be certain that competing cricketers will not relax and can prevent any complacency in a player by protracting the competition. It may not be comforting to the cricketers but it makes for combative efficiency, and it can be reasonably assumed that Yorkshire have more than once taken that pragmatic view.

Little if any of this was in Fred Trueman's mind on the evening of 10 May, 1949 when he met the rest of the Yorkshire team – all of them except Brian Close complete strangers to him – at the Danum Hotel at Doncaster for the journey to Cambridge.

He has said that when he went on to the field at Fenners next morning he was nervous for the only time in his life. Perhaps that was the beginning of the transformation of the basic Fred Trueman. He – probably only he – sensed that he had ceased to be an ordinary boy.

CHAPTER THREE

Colt

Even Yorkshire have rarely given a first appearance in the same match to three young cricketers of such ultimate distinction as Brian Close, Frank Lowson and Fred Trueman who were in their eleven against Cambridge University on 11 May, 1949. All were to become Test players. Close and Lowson both won their county caps in that season, when Close also became the youngest man both to perform the 'double' and to play for England. Trueman did not yet achieve so much; but, though he was not aware of it, his personal mythology began.

He opened the bowling for Yorkshire: and that single first ball was achievement: but, on a typically easy Fenners pitch of the type he later came to hate bitterly and eloquently, he could find no bounce: trying to bowl too fast, he lost his rhythm and, with it, most of his control and pace as well. He was, too, no-balled for dragging his back foot over the line of the bowling crease which seemed to him at the time the least of his troubles. To his relief he delivered an occasional ball near the point and pace he intended so, when Yorkshire won easily, his figures of three wickets – including the boast-worthy one of Hubert Doggart, clean bowled – for ninety-four runs did not disgrace him: perhaps, indeed, they flattered him a little. Few young fast bowlers make any deep impression at Fenners; in later years it was a case-hardened Trueman who proved such an awkward proposition there. None of the Cambridge players saw anything remarkable in his pace but some recall him proceeding to the nets with an aged, heavy bat, dark brown in colour, and bearing – burnt deeply into the back – the words MALTBY MAIN C.C. The elder of the Yorkshire school, Herbert Sutcliffe, appeared to pass a professional eye over the three young players and his genteel accent was in strong contrast to that of the enthusiastic and deeply Yorkshire-sounding Trueman who communicated to him his determination to become 'fastest bloody bowler in t'world'.

It is related, too, that at The University Arms, he was presented with a menu in French and, pointing to the words at the bottom – Jeudi le douzième Mai – said 'Ay, ah'll have that for sweet'. The first words of the Trueman saga had been uttered.

Wisden noted that 'Yorkshire gave a trial to three young players, Lowson, an opening batsman, Close an all-rounder and Trueman a spin bowler.' That word 'spin' hurt – even at a year's range.

The Parks pitch for the Oxford University match was livelier than at Fenners. Trueman's mentors impressed on him that he must not strain for pace and the steadying influence of Coxon at the other end helped him to bowl with his true rhythm. In two bursts in the first innings he took four for 31; and was fast enough to impress himself on the memories of some of his opponents. Clive van Rynefeld was 'in' and batting with some confidence when, as he aimed to play Trueman in the direction of mid-on, a late out-swinger flung his off stump out of the ground. Altogether he had six wickets for 72: but, while Lowson and Close were retained for the following match, Trueman was not.

There was simply no place for him in the team, so long as Aspinall and Coxon were fit with Close – worth his place as a batsman – and Norman Yardley to bowl swing at need.

Aspinall had taken thirty wickets in three matches and had been picked for the Test Trial before, late in May, he ruptured an Achilles tendon so severely that he was never again able to bowl effectively. In that moment Yorkshire's strategy was seriously disorganised: cricket history – and, though no one realized it, Fred Trueman's life – took a fresh course. Since neither Whitehead nor Foord was available, the player chosen to replace Aspinall was Frank McHugh – who later went to Gloucestershire – a tall bowler of rather slavish in-swing but with some pace from the pitch. In a run of three matches he made little impression apart from sharing an early breakthrough with Coxon against Derbyshire, and Trueman was brought in for the Whitsun fixture with Lancashire. The Old Trafford pitch was slow: neither Trueman, Coxon nor Dick Pollard – who opened the Lancashire bowling – took even one wicket and, in Yorkshire's next match, Close shared the new ball with Coxon. The following fixture, against the Minor Counties, at Lord's, was outside the Championship: so seven first-team players were rested and Trueman was given another chance.

The game went along steadily and unremarkably on a pitch which granted some turn, so that the spinners took most of the wickets in the first three innings until, on the third day, the Minor Counties needed 272 to win. In the first of his great bursts, Fred Trueman took five wickets for 30 runs in a nine-over spell before lunch. Norman Yardley bowled him all through the innings, with only the luncheon interval for a break. His final figures for the innings were eight for 70: *Wisden* referred to him on this occasion as fast-medium; and he had implanted his name in some influential minds at Lord's.

Still erratic and hasty in his use of the bouncer, he was a wicket-keeper's nightmare; nevertheless Don Brennan, who had to do an alarming amount of diving wide to leg side and off to counter his vagaries of line, recalls that he was always grateful for a catch taken, and never reproachful about one dropped.

He played on and off until early July when he was peremptorily dropped after the Surrey match at Bradford. The Yorkshire Committee has always had a reputation for chilling self-satisfaction in its young players. There is little doubt, though, that at this time they simply, and reasonably, did not think

Trueman was a good enough bowler for them. He offended their sense of economy. Their success had always been based on tight out-cricket. They could hardly feel enthusiastic about a young fast bowler who – in complete contrast to the later Trueman – was as likely as not to play in a new batsman by giving him a wide long-hop as his first ball. He might murder Minor Counties batsmen, but when Championship points were at issue he was regularly costing three and a half runs an over. He took four wickets against Surrey but they scored off him at a rate of nearly six an over – which Yorkshire found intolerable in their opening bowler. Foord and Whitehead could bowl accurately and tactically: the committee made a special request to Foord's headmaster to release him for a fortnight and he took Trueman's place.

Some who know Trueman most closely believe that Yorkshire Committee's decisions in this summer and the next were an important, and by no means happy, formative influence on his character.

Bill Foord, was contemplating giving up, or at least suspending, his career as a schoolmaster to become a professional cricketer: and Yorkshire were interested to keep in close touch with him. He bowled tidily but unremarkably in three matches until John Whitehead came down from University and took over.

The match at Bramall Lane against the New Zealanders carried no points and Coxon took the rest he had earned, while Trueman and Whitehead opened the bowling in collaboration and competition. Fred's mother, father, brothers and sisters were there to watch. The outcome was predictable – almost inevitable – Fred Trueman, in the effort to blast Whitehead out of contention, wrenched a thigh muscle: he was carried off the field, and could not play again that season.

Unlike the other sixteen cricketing counties, Yorkshire, with their numerous grounds, have no real home where the players regularly foregather or have permanent lockers; and even Leeds was far from Fred Trueman's home at Maltby. So he could only stay there, feeling miserably forgotten, as Whitehead occasionally replaced Foord in the bowling place he had so eagerly aspired to fill. Meanwhile Yorkshire won seven of their last eight matches to come from well down the table and share the Championship title with Middlesex.

They did not simply do it without him: they did it without giving a word, a sign or – so far as he could guess – a thought to him. That experience changed him; his belief in himself as a fast bowler never wavered, but he needed his father's constant reassurances to relieve his feeling of bitterness and injury: and always afterwards there was something of a chip on his shoulder, a mistrust of authority, a feeling that, if he did not watch them, 'they' would do him some injustice.

Certainly, in the years that followed, he seemed at times to be given less than his due recognition. Did he bridle too quickly, anticipate a slight or an injustice? Whatever the reason, his former extravagant, but open, friendly, boisterousness became charged with a degree of resentment which could make him uncomfortable company for those he did not trust. Those who won his respect had no such experience, for, once he was convinced of anyone's goodwill, he could be quite vulnerably trusting. To such understanding and help as he had from Cyril Turner, Bill Bowes, Maurice Leyland and Arthur Mitchell, he responded with loyalty and affection.

Henceforward, too, a former trait became exaggerated; he had always been something of an extrovert, likely to speak before he thought. Now he developed an almost pathological need to talk, a demand for an audience which stemmed from ill-ease. He could be silent with those he knew intimately and trusted; with strangers he was a compulsive – though often amusing – talker.

In his first season he had played eight matches and taken thirty-one wickets, thirteen in his four Championship games. When he went back to the winter coaching classes at Leeds,

seeds of doubt had been planted: his coaches were not satisfied
with his summer's work: yet, there, to settle at least some of
their uncertainty, was that superb action. They went to work
again; and so did he, but the former boyish cheerfulness had
been replaced by an altogether grimmer determination.

The steadying and coordinating process was slow, and often
disappointing to those who saw most merit in him. He played
little for the Second XI: when he was not wanted by the county,
local practice usually directed that he was farmed out to some
Yorkshire Council side. Against the opposition he met there he
was terrifying. Appreciably faster than any other bowler most of
his opponents had ever seen, he was wayward in both length
and direction, and considered the element of fear justified in
his method. He gloried in being fast, tough and ruthless, and in
hating batsmen.

When he played for the county he was not happy. While his
hunger for cricket was still insatiable, and his determination
firm, he was out of tune with his team-mates. Yorkshire in 1950
were strong in batting but they probably lost the Championship
for lack of a fast bowler and a second finger spinner. Trueman
saw his chance but he could not take it, in part because he was
over-eager; largely because he simply was not good enough – he
still lacked the physical strength to satisfy himself in speed, and
his critics in control – but also to a marked extent because of
lack of personal encouragement. When he succeeded no one
seemed to share his pleasure: when he failed he resented both
his failure and the atmosphere in which it happened.

The Yorkshire dressing room of the 1950s was not a happy
place. A subsequent player, who knew it only in its late days
once said – 'Never be surprised if Fred seems to play for himself
– nearly everyone in the team did when he started'. The record
is a sad one: Johnnie Wardle was dismissed for 'unsatisfactory
behaviour'; Alec Coxon, of whom it was said that 'his face did
not fit', Brian Stott, Ken Taylor and Frank Lowson all retired
while they were still capable of more and valuable years of first-

class play. One captain – Billy Sutcliffe – and one captain-presumptive, in Geoffrey Keighley, withdrew. Willie Watson and Ray Illingworth, both Test players, left to play for other counties. Norman Yardley, for all his ability as a player and tactical acumen as a captain, was an easy-going person and by no means always in complete control of the senior players, nor able to quell the rancours or reconcile the strong antipathies of the dressing room. One of his players described him as 'too nice a chap to be the skipper we need' while another commented that the team had 'too many captains'.

It is probable that, if they had enjoyed their cricket with the county, both Norman Yardley and Len Hutton might have continued longer than they did: as elder figures they could have contributed much to the team in skill, experience, and tradition. In the event, Trueman proved the most durable of them all, except Close who, though he lasted longer, suffered in his turn a savage and unexpected stroke of the axe.

It should be noted that, in the twenty-one years spanned by the career of Close and almost by that of Trueman, Yorkshire won the County Championship seven times, and shared it once. The team of the early 1950s, though, has no share in those achievements: after sharing the title with Middlesex in 1949, the county were not Champions until 1959, which represents their longest period without a win since their first modern Championship in 1893.

The Fred Trueman who stepped with the bravado of un-certainty into that dressing room was young, uncapped, gauche and unsophisticated. He wore shaggy jackets and garish ties; and he was noisy: senior players tended not to be amused by him, preferring the company and the conversation of others more mature and quieter. Several times he considered leaving the county and, for one of his strong Yorkshire loyalties, that argues a savage degree of disenchantment. Some of his troubles were due to his own naïvete. He was insensitive in matters like talking to a taut batsman waiting to go in, or someone who had just made a duck. He wanted to enjoy his cricket, and life: he wanted a lot of fun, often of a kind too rowdy for some of his seniors. He cracked jokes to people when they did not want jokes. Since he was generally the junior member of the team, and uncapped, he could be 'put in his place' by anyone else in the dressing room and he frequently was – and rarely gently. He was hasty; and quick to take – or imagine – offence: and in protesting against it he did not hesitate to employ the most potent nouns, verbs and adjectives in the language.

Most of all he wanted to be reassured. He wanted people to tell him he was good; and the rest of the players – some older and disinterested, others, like him, struggling to make a place in the side and in need of comfort themselves – were sadistic as professional competitors often are. They might think he was fast, but they would never say so; only observe wrily 'Now, if you were as quick as Alec Coxon. . . .' 'Johnnie Whitehead is going to make a real quickie' or 'Why do you take that long run up? – you run faster than the ball'. He was slow to realise that a county cricket team was not a family: that he was in a world where honest confession of self-doubt and disinterested kindness were considered as weakness. Many years afterwards he recalled that in those days of bitter surprise only John Whitehead, his rival bowler, stood up for him. His instinctive openness made him vulnerable. He resolved to close the gap, play it hard, and for some time it seemed that he had managed to do so: his flashes of indignation could be daunting. Eventually some subconscious process ensured that those who failed to tell him he was good found he was telling them – and in detail. In 1950, though, that relief lay distant in the future.

Norman Yardley, who first viewed the brash youngster with the thick South Yorkshire accent in some surprise, soon came to treat him with cheerful humour. As a joke he christened him 'Fiery Freddie'; and often put him on to bowl with the words 'I think a spot of Fiery is called for'. On the other hand, he was always a cheerful, considerate captain: and serious and helpful

c

on tactical matters. 'This chap is bound to play forward to your
first ball' – 'Don't drop short to this man' – 'Give him a bouncer'
– 'Keep away from the leg stump' : he would remember, too,
to say 'Well bowled'. Fred was always easier to coax than drive.
If there were too many disparities between them for any close
friendship to exist, mutual respect developed, and Fred remains
grateful for those early kindnesses.

He was still working in the pit and frequently had to take
on night shifts to play cricket by day; he was conscious of this
as a disadvantage – and as a social handicap, too – by comparison with the other players. Increasingly often he simply took
time off and eventually he was called up into the RAF. In
1950, though, he was still living at home in Maltby: and he
and his father looked forward to the cricket season with un-
dimmed faith in his fast-bowling.

He was left out of the county's first two matches; picked for
the Cambridge University game, in which not a ball was bowled
because of rain; and against the West Indies, when his vagaries
were too great a risk in a low-scoring match. 'Norman Yardley
soon had to tell me to put my sweater on, and I was far from
happy about my own bowling'. He had only four overs in the
first innings, one in the second.

He expected trouble but he was retained in the side to play
Gloucestershire, at Bristol where he found some comfort in
taking six wickets, all from the upper part of the batting order.
Even in his most extravagant hopes, though, he could not have
anticipated the fact that, without doing anything else comparable, he was picked for the Rest against England in the Test
Trial at the end of May.

He had no sustained figures or performances to justify selection at that level. In truth he was chosen because the selectors –
R. E. S. Wyatt, Brian Sellers, Tom Pearce and Leslie Ames –
with their minds on the repeated downfall of the English batsmen before Miller and Lindwall were concerned to give them
practice against pace. Perhaps subconsciously, they also reflected

public feeling, the national desire for a fast bowler, even an inexperienced one – anyone so long as he was fast. If Trueman was not yet widely known, no one else had given comparable evidence or promise of pace: Brian Statham did not make his first appearance for Lancashire until a few weeks later.

Trueman was still an uncapped Yorkshire player when he went to the historic Test Trial, played on a turning Park Avenue wicket, where Jim Laker had his amazing analysis of eight wickets for two runs. The Rest were put out for 27, the lowest total ever recorded in a representative match. Trueman – stumped Evans, bowled A. Bedser 1 – at least escaped a 'duck'; but, to his disappointment, was not given the new ball at the start of the England innings. Hubert Doggart, captain of the Rest, put on Les Jackson at one end but he chose to use Eric Bedser, bowling off breaks, from the end Laker had used. Jenkins and Berry, too, were given spells of spin before Trueman came on. He had nine overs and, to his immense pride, bowled Len Hutton – whose batting he admired without qualification, despite subsequent differences – with an inswinger. England did not need a second innings so if Trueman, who had caught Norman Yardley off Jenkins, left without having made any impression at least he had done his interests no harm.

He still could not bowl tight, often not even straight on batsmen's wickets: sometimes not on bowlers' either. After his return to Yorkshire, ten expensive wickets in four games did not compensate for undisciplined bowling which allowed three-and-a-half, even four, runs an over. As soon as John White-head could be free, he was brought in and, in his second match, had five Essex wickets for 50. In the next three weeks Trueman had only one county match – against Derbyshire on the traditional pace-bowlers' wicket at Chesterfield – when he was given second use of the new ball after Coxon and Whitehead. His desperation was reflected in four 'called' wides and a number of border-line cases: but in the end he and Whitehead had similar analyses. Their longer term – though crucially, not their runs-per-over rates – were again alike when Whitehead was injured and Trueman replaced him for the away game with Nottinghamshire.

In later years Fred Trueman produced some fine performances at Trent Bridge – one at least of considerable significance in his career – and it is tempting to wonder, in view of the incalculable factors that sometimes triggered his great spells, whether they were inspired by his wretched experience there in 1950.

It was the first instance of the distressing condition he simply called 'stitch' which seriously and unpredictably affected his bowling from time to time in his early years. The pitch, as usual, was perfect for batting; the redoubtable Charles Harris delighted to seize verbal and psychological advantage over a fast bowler – especially a young one from Yorkshire – and his partner, Walter Keeton, was quick to join in plundering some ill-directed and not particularly fast bowling.

The spinners, Wardle and Leadbeater took over, Yorkshire won by an innings and 124 runs: but Trueman's nine first innings overs – he did not bowl in the second – cost 58 runs. It was announced to the press that he was unfit for the next match because of a strained side and this time he was left alone in Maltby with his angry thoughts for six weeks.

John Whitehead walked into the vacant place, with, to all appearances, the open invitation to make it his own. He failed to do so: and so, with less incentive or opportunity, did Foord. Although no one realised it at the time, it was then that the banished Trueman, without bowling a ball, drew ahead of them both.

Again his father faithfully convinced him that this long silence did not represent the final dismissal he feared – for Yorkshire's loose arrangement with uncapped players involved no contract, retaining fee nor even communication.

The all but unemployed fast-bowler had much to think about. He knew a number of the other players disliked him, found him rough, talked about him behind his back, and would not regret his absence. He missed the money, too; eighteen pounds a match gave a useful lift to his personal life; but above all, his aspirations had been checked: and his pride was hurt. He knew, too, and at last admitted it fully to himself, that his obsession with speed had endangered his career as a bowler.

If tentative hints that he might join Lancashire, Surrey or Sussex had taken firmer shape, he would happily have left Yorkshire at this time. He was himself to become a symbol of Yorkshire, of Yorkshire aggression and Yorkshire cricket; but he had found the atmosphere of their cricket harsh. There was, too, the attitude of their opponents. The gregarious Trueman, strolling into the other side's dressing room to chat, discovered to his surprise that a special hostility seemed to exist towards his county. He attributed this feeling to the Yorkshire teams of the inter-war period. In his own words 'They were the outstanding county and they beat everyone out of sight but from what I can make out, they were bad devils, too, and they made a lot of enemies among the players who were to become coaches after the war'.

He turned all this in his mind during those six weeks while Whitehead, and occasionally Foord, took the county place he felt to be his; and he was not even asked to play for the second team. Some innocent and rather apprehensive club batsmen bore the explosive brunt of his smouldering displeasure. So, when he was at length recalled, it was no repentant prodigal who came back for the last two Championship matches, but a rather resentful young man still satisfied of his ability to succeed at cricket; and still wanting the money: but now determined – as he was to remain all his cricketing life – to bloody well show them. Whether the emphasis should be on 'show', or on the anti-Trueman 'them' may be debated.

The first of the two matches, against Glamorgan, was ruined by rain; in the second, when Yorkshire beat Hampshire by an innings, Trueman had three useful wickets and bowled with improved control. He was not asked to play in the social affair against MCC in the Scarborough Festival. In the county bowling averages he finished eighth – behind Appleyard, Wardle, Coxon, Mason, Smales, Yardley and Leadbeater – with thirty wickets. That was the same number in Championship matches as Whitehead, but Trueman's were four runs apiece cheaper, at 28. In due course he was summoned back to the winter shed at Leeds where his coaches were waiting to tell him, and convince him of the finality of the judgement that he was now prepared to recognise – there was no future for him as a Yorkshire bowler if he did not maintain the county's standards of accuracy and economy. He listened, practised and, otherwise, worked in the pit, played some football, kept himself fit and looked aggressively and warily to the future.

CHAPTER FOUR

Firm Foothold

Mounting physical strength, a slight increase in height, diligent winter practice, his father's unfailing encouragement, and, above all, his acceptance of the need to set control before pace, sent Fred Trueman better equipped, as well as more adult, to the season of 1951 than ever before. The retirement of Alec Coxon at the end of 1950 could not be explained on grounds of performance; he had finished effectively seventh in the national averages with 131 wickets at 18.6: they said in the dressing-room, uneasily, that 'his face didn't fit'. Any idea that his absence automatically made Trueman a certain first team player was dispelled by the knowledge that the medium-paced Bob Appleyard, who had been 'blooded' in the previous season, was expected to win a regular place. In the event, Appleyard dominated not only Yorkshire's, but the entire first-class bowling for the season with 200 wickets at 14.14. Moreover it was known that, when John Whitehead left London in mid-season, he would have completed his degree course and be ready to play regularly.

Trueman, picked for the four most serious of the county's first six matches, generally came off better than Foord who played only in three non-Championship fixtures and intimated that he had now decided to put teaching before cricket. Trueman did little in Yorkshire's heavy defeat by MCC but, after taking one South African wicket for three runs on a spinners' pitch in the first innings, he routed their team of Test standard in the second. He took five for 19 in fifteen overs and all but broke the last wicket stand that, at 96 for nine, saved the touring side from an innings defeat.

His early figures consistently argued greater penetration and accuracy than before; and such analyses as three for 16, three for 23 and five for 93 ensured that, when one of the faster bowlers was omitted, he was the one retained to take the new ball with the practically irresistible Appleyard. He was now too wise to believe himself secure. His five for 93 was the product of only nineteen overs, the run rate barely pardonable although he had taken wickets: but he had no excuse for 53 runs and only one – tail end – wicket in the second innings. Then, as if he sensed Whitehead at his shoulder, he began to press and, against Middlesex at Lord's he bowled fifteen overs for 66 runs and not a wicket. Surely enough, John Whitehead was ready for the next match: he, Trueman and Appleyard were included in the team to play Notts at Bramall Lane. It was all too much like some unpleasant film loop coming round for the third time: the same ground as that of his injury in 1949; the same opponents as those of his disaster in 1950. Sheffield is the ground nearest Maltby and his father offered his usual encouragement: but only the bowler himself could ensure that neither anxiety, bitterness nor over-straining should impair performance.

In the first innings Whitehead, described as 'our new and most promising fast bowler' in a book by Norman Yardley which did not mention Trueman (who, of course, was bristlingly aware of the fact) was given the new ball with Appleyard. He took two for 35; Trueman, first change, three for 26. When Notts batted again, wanting 164 to save an innings defeat, they were unlikely to make the runs, but time lost to rain meant that Yorkshire had only the last – short – afternoon to bowl them out. The pitch now was soft on top and hard underneath and Trueman, opening the bowling with Whitehead, made the ball rise angrily and often enough to prompt some hasty movement by the batsmen. Not so long before, the sight of the ball flying so spectacularly would have incited him to every wild extravagance of pace and over-indulgence in the bouncer. Now he used the lifting ball only as a tactical variation. He bowled straight enough to hit the stumps five times, had a second innings analysis of eight wickets for 68 in 20.8 overs (Whitehead took two for 47 in 16): eleven for 94 in the match and effectively gave Yorkshire their innings win.

The rest of the team stood back and applauded as Trueman, his sweater thrown about his shoulders, ran up the pavilion steps. He had never had a cricket moment like this before. Such a day must surely, he felt, have finally decided the issue between him and Whitehead. He recalls that in those few moments he envisaged the possibility of being chosen for the Old Trafford Test against South Africa in the following week. He took the few steps and the quick turn into the dressing room and, as he crossed to his peg, caught sight of the team sheet for the next match, pinned up by the fireplace. His name was not on it. He was to join the second eleven who were playing Lincolnshire at Grimsby the next day. His spluttering and murderously worded amazement elicited from Norman Yardley the explanation that the team had been picked early in the afternoon so that it could be announced to the press: that the selection committee had considered the three men returning from the Test Match (two batsmen and a spin bowler): that John Whitehead was available: and that he – Trueman – had not been bowling well lately.

Torn between anger and the most bitter disappointment he had yet known in cricket, he went to Grimsby, where he was not even asked to play for the second team but was made twelfth man, and had to watch Bill Foord take seven for 35. If he had been unduly proud of himself after his performance against Notts, he had certainly been taken down a peg; or, if the intent was to stir him to high pace, it proved successful. Recalled to the first team, he took eighteen wickets in four out of five games: Whitehead, who had thirteen in five was left out for the return with Notts at Trent Bridge.

At last luck broke for Trueman. The first morning was hazy and the pitch green. Norman Yardley won the toss, put Notts in and, with 'Help yourself, Fiery' turned him loose. Making the ball swing late at clinking pace, he tore out the off stumps of Reggie Simpson and Alan Armitage, and had Peter Harvey caught at the wicket, with successive balls – the first hat-trick by a Yorkshire player for five years. At one point Notts were 18 for six wickets and Trueman had taken four of them: he won the match and his final figures, eight for 53, were the best of his career until then.

With improved control and reinforced by success, he was beginning to bowl to Norman Yardley's direction with point as well as effort. His six wickets (including the first five batsmen) for 59 in a Derbyshire innings of 339 on a good batting pitch at Harrogate was not only remarkably penetrative, but a thrifty piece of bowling. Performed in twenty-seven overs it was the most convincing evidence he had yet produced of his developing tactical perception and ability.

Within a fortnight he had proved – and disproved – some conflicting opinions about himself: now others, too, knew he was a fast bowler. After a couple more quite undistinguished games, on 13 August, at Park Avenue, Bradford, Norman Yardley awarded Yorkshire caps to Appleyard – who expected one – and to Trueman, who considered he deserved it but would not believe he had it until it was in his hand. He took only seven wickets in Yorkshire's remaining six matches, most of which, in that wet August, were played on spinners' pitches.

Bob Appleyard was already mature by cricketing age-standards at twenty-six, when he first appeared for Yorkshire in two matches of 1950. No one could then have guessed at the extent of his success in 1951 when, so far as Yorkshire were concerned, he replaced both the departed Coxon and Close who was away on National Service. Over six feet tall, he bowled medium-paced swingers with the new ball; on a turning pitch, or when the shine had gone, he employed slow to slow-medium off-spin and cut, with extensive variations of flight and pace. Now, in his first full season he took 200 wickets – more than anyone else in England – at 14.4 and, apart from Ramadhin's figures from a single festival match, was top of the first-class bowling averages. He was not physically strong, yet he was always so anxious to bowl that his captains frequently found it difficult to take him off. He did not like batsmen, nor Fred Trueman. In this year an attack of pleurisy put him out of the Yorkshire-South Africans game and kept him from the county's next two fixtures when he had taken 99 wickets, and surely prevented him being the first bowler in the country to the hundred. Because of illness he played only one match in 1952 and none in 1953; missed half the 1955 season and left the game in 1958. Nevertheless, in barely five full seasons he took more than 700 wickets for an average of 15; one can only guess what he might have achieved had he been fully fit.

Trueman turned out against MCC in the Scarborough Festival – when he first met his future wife – and at last was admitted to the social sector of the county's cricket. He finished the season with ninety wickets for 20.57: Whitehead had twenty-four at 20.08. Their particular contest was over and John Whitehead joined Worcestershire. A complete episode of Fred Trueman's life had been acted out. He had reached a goal he knew he could attain when others doubted it. He was there now: no one could take it away: he had shown them. Rolling his heavy shoulders inside his jacket, he resolved to show them more.

As soon as the season ended he began his National Service with the RAF and, after his initial training, was posted to Hemswell in Lincolnshire first as AC 2, rising later to AC 1. It was not an arduous life; his duties consisted of looking after the sports equipment store and the football and cricket pitches. His football, at centre forward, was capable enough for Lincoln City to invite him to sign on and play for their junior team. He had learnt the truth of the adage that a Yorkshire cap is hard to win. Now, with plenty of exercise and a companionable life, respected by his fellow aircraftsmen from Yorkshire because he had played cricket for the county, and unworried, he relaxed, grew taller, filled out and flexed his muscles with the unaccustomed feeling that the world, at last, was beginning to recognise him for the man he believed he was.

CHAPTER FIVE

The Fast Bowler

The peace-time RAF could be flexible with its National Service men and, though Trueman could not be released regularly for Yorkshire, he could keep in practice by playing for his unit, the RAF or the Combined Services. Meanwhile it was understood that, if he was wanted for a Test Match – or even a trial to show his paces for the selectors – he would be allowed the necessary time off.

Naturally enough, he studied the cricket scores in the newspapers, watchful for rivals or successors. He need not have worried: ironically enough now, when he was not available, Yorkshire positively needed him for the first time. Alec Coxon had gone (and the county must have wished they still had him): Bob Appleyard was ill, Foord and Whitehead took no part and, for the opening matches with MCC, and the two Universities, George Padgett, Brian Hall and Mike Cownley were all given trial runs as opening bowlers. So, as the season wore on, were Eric Burgin, Bill Holdsworth, Peter Brayshay and George Cawthray; but by then Fred Trueman had climbed far beyond their challenge and to greater heights than even he had dared to expect so soon.

It is difficult for later generations to appreciate quite what Fred Trueman meant in 1952, not simply as a performer but as a symbol – heroic, epic, nostalgic, dramatic, comic and downright earthy – constituted exactly to the demand of the day. Many of those who returned to an everyday peace-time existence in Britain after the second World War regarded cricket as the confirmation of normality, the promise that all was again well; that men might busy themselves gravely about unimportant matters. In 1947 the feats of Edrich and Compton kept enthusiasm alight and in 1948 came Bradman's Australians, personified by Lindwall and Miller, the contrastingly splendid fast bowlers who destroyed the English batting with the sweeping completeness of a forest fire. When they took the new ball – and under the 65-over Law of those days such moments were not far apart – a hush fell on the ground such as can be felt at the crisis of a great play. The only British sporting parallel of recent times is the chill that descended on Wembley Stadium in November 1953 when a 100,000 people simultaneously sensed that they were about to see the legendary dominance of English football tumbled headlong by a new – or forgotten – power now poised in the hands of Hungary.

There were few in cricketing England who did not admire, and even relish, the superb mastery of the two Australian fast bowlers; but the more they admired them, the more they yearned for England to possess such a force, so that the Australian batting, too, might be harried and routed.

Possible candidates for this St George-like task were sought with more hope than certainty. There was Ken Preston, of Essex – but he broke a leg: P. A. Whitcombe the tall young Oxford Blue – but Bill Brown hooked him into the Tavern as if he were bowling with a tennis ball: there were many more, like Trueman's two rivals, Foord and Whitehead of Yorkshire; Tom Hall, who went from Derbyshire to Somerset; even the Scotsman, R. S. Hodge of Greenock and Fifeshire, was canvassed. The fact was that they were all good-hearted fast-medium; not one of them could have parted the hair of an Australian batsman – which was the purpose of the search – and it was doubtful if any of them matched the pace of the pre-war survivors, Bill Copson and Alf Gover.

That was understandable in the immediate post-war years but now six seasons had passed since the first-class game re-

started and still the avenging fast bowler had not materialised.
Word of Trueman had spread round cricketing circles since
his first appearance. In his early days, especially when he was
dropped by Yorkshire, the subject was smothered under such
comments as 'No, no, too wild altogether' or 'Raw, you know,
probably never come to anything'. He was always worth a look
and a paragraph through 1949: his selection for the Test Trial
brought him back into the news in 1950: he faded out again
when he lost his county place: but in 1951 there could no
longer be any doubt that Yorkshire had capped a genuinely
fast bowler. Whether he was England material or not was debated. One group of critics presented him as the new Larwood
(after 'the second Bradman' the most dangerous of all cricket
labels) while the other cited his past inaccuracies and preached
patience.

Patience was not popular. Some knowledgeable observers who
had watched his progress with interest and hope thought he was
not ready; but it could be sensed that, in a unique way, not
merely involved cricketers – but an immense number of people
who were simply aware that Test Matches were played between England and Australia – wanted Trueman; or at least,
they wanted a fast-bowler and, in its rarely unanimous, but
intuitive way, the public mind had settled on Trueman.

It seemed as if the selectors, in unusually democratic fashion,
set out to collect sufficient evidence to pick Trueman for Eng-
and. Trueman's station commander proved cooperative and
released him for Yorkshire's early, miniature – four-match –
home season at Huddersfield, Bradford, Bramall Lane and
Headingley, against Somerset, Worcestershire, Derbyshire and
Lancashire.

No one, not even Fred himself, realised the full extent of his
physical and psychological development since he had been in
the RAF. He had gone there a wild fast bowler; by the following spring he was probably the fastest bowler in the world:
certainly he himself is convinced that his pace was never so

high for any sustained period either before or after. The first time that summer he took up the ball in earnest he reduced Somerset to two for two wickets – Gimblett bowled and Stephenson caught at the wicket – out of an eventual six for 65. Hampered by stiffness in the second innings he took two for 44: Yorkshire won by an innings and 32 in two days. Cricket was not work to him; it simply bubbled out of him.

At Bradford, after Yorkshire had demonstrated the excellence of the pitch for batting by scoring 399 on the first day, he began the second by hurling out the first five Worcestershire batsmen – players as good as Don Kenyon, Peter Richardson, Laddie Outschoorn, Ronnie Bird and Bob Broadbent – four of them clean bowled – in nineteen balls for five runs; he took three more wickets, made two catches and again Yorkshire, without needing to bat a second time, won with more than a day to spare. After that the selectors could not have left him out of the England team if they had wanted to. Such an idea did not enter their heads. In any event when Yorkshire achieved their third innings win – against Derbyshire – although it was played on a slow pitch, more suitable for spinners, he had five for 107 in the match: and four for 86 in the Whitsun draw with Lancashire.

So, with thirty-two wickets at 14.2 each from four County Championship games, he went to his first Test Match. It was no trouble: it was played on the very ground where he had just finished the Roses Match. With an awe he strove not to show, he joined the England team in their Harrogate hotel for dinner and the pre-match discussion. Some of them drank beer: he was still a teetotaller: he sipped his orange squash and had no fear whatever for the match.

Fred Trueman, in June 1952, was at his physical peak: he had developed so rapidly during the recent few months that he had all the instinctive confidence of one who is as fit, game and battle-tuned as a fighting cock.

He was now twenty-one years old and, importantly, he had

The Colt

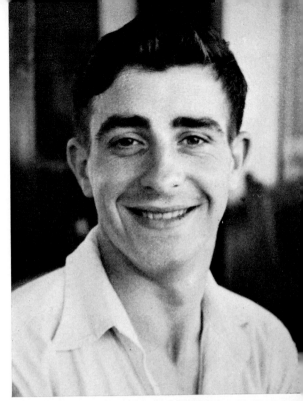

The Fast Bowler

A great catch after 'going the wrong way', to dismiss Miller off Laker, Leeds 1956

suddenly grown taller, to an ideal height, for a fast bowler, of five-feet-ten. This brought him the fresh and crucial advantage of being able to dig the ball in, as opposed to skidding through : yet he was still sufficiently compact in proportion to avoid the stresses of the over-tall. He measured forty-six inches round both the chest and the hips; and he weighed thirteen-and-a-half stone. These measurements changed little through his playing career and they are those of a powerfully built man. He has been likened physically to Harold Larwood but in fact he was quite significantly bigger. When Larwood first played for England, also at the age of twenty-one, he was five-feet-seven-and-a-half tall and his weight was ten-stone-eight; he, too, maintained roughly the same proportions throughout his bowling days.

Fred Trueman had, and still has, immensely strong legs which probably accounted, to a considerable extent, for his remarkable stamina and long career. He had also, as his measurements indicate, strong hips and, as a fast bowler needs to cushion the jolt of delivery, a wide stern. Jim Swanton, remarking on that fact as he passed Fred lying on the massage table, was halted by the instant retort 'A big spike needs a big hammer to drive it home'. Apart from a tendency to 'stitch' which passed soon in his playing life, the back injury he suffered in 1950, an ankle turned in a deep foot-pit in 1952, and a couple of instances of blistered heels, he rarely missed a match through injury or unfitness over twenty years: a remarkable record for a really fast and hard-worked bowler. In his early days his drag used to rip open the toes of as many as nine cricket boots a season, and he had some pain from the jolt of his left foot in the delivery stride. As a result he had specially steel-toed, strengthened and cushioned boots designed and made for him and, though he went through them at a fair rate, he never approached the former figure of nine a season.

In 1952 he came to his peak of speed. He already had a well hidden slower ball, commanded a menacing bumper, given responsive conditions he made his out-swinger 'go' very late, and

D

sometimes, though less often, produced an in-swinger. He was to add many refinements and subtleties and increase his stamina with the years: but Len Hutton, who had observed him as closely as anyone – and perhaps more astutely – thought him still dangerously immature: and, in fact, prophesied accurately the period of his fullest and most effective maturity. He agreed, however, that Trueman never bowled faster than in 1952. Sheer pace is not the criterion of a fast bowler: he was at his fastest, not his best: but to be the fastest in the country was for him the realisation of a dream.

This was not only the most exciting season of his life, it was one of the most exciting any cricketer has ever known although, apart from five Championship matches for Yorkshire and four Tests, he played only in services games. Those few matches made him internationally known, not only as a cricketer, but also as a personality. He was not alone in finding it stimulating for, to cricketing England, he became the long-sought fast bowler who should at last carry the battle to Australia. Brian Statham had been flown out as a replacement on the MCC 1950-1 tour of Australia: Alec Bedser, whose pace was honest fast-medium, had carried an immense burden of work for six years; but neither had seized the public imagination as this dark-haired, brown-eyed, pale-faced, heavy-shouldered Yorkshireman now did.

His run-up in his early days was more than a pitch-length long: at least twenty-two measured paces and then, as a rule, three or four walking steps thrown in for launching purposes : sometimes, too, he went an extra few strides nearer the sight-screen for the non-benefit of nervous batsmen. The actual approach, though, was of thirteen running strides. In later years, when he was less concerned with speed, he often used a run of only thirteen measured paces.

At his fastest, off the long run, he moved up in a curve, swerving slightly out, round the umpire. His coaches had adjusted a few details of his action but fundamentally it was as natural as it was splendid. He stalked back to his mark, arms bowed, at a threateningly muscle-bound gait: but as soon as he gathered himself and began his run he became a different creature. About this time someone described him as a young bull; and there was in his approach that majestic rhythm that emerges as a surprise in the Spanish fighting bull. It steps out of the toril, stands hesitant, cumbersome then, suddenly, sights the peon from the cuadrilla, pulls itself up and sets off towards him in a mounting glory of rhythm, power and majesty. Such was the run up of the young Trueman as, body thrown forward, he moved first at a steady pad and gradually accelerated, hair flopping, and swept into the delivery process. Again the analogy of the bull holds good, for the peak of its charge is controlled violence, precisely applied in a movement of rippling speed. Trueman's body swung round so completely that the batsman saw his left shoulder blade: the broad left foot was, for an infinitesimal period of time, poised to hammer the ground. He was a cocked trigger, left arm pointed high, head steady, eyes glaring at the batsman as that great stride widened . the arm slashed down and as the ball was fired down the pitch, his body was thrown hungrily after it, the right toe raking the ground closely beside the wicket as he swept on. Coming in almost from behind the umpire threw his left shoulder up and helped him to deliver from so near the stumps that sometimes he brushed the umpire. Indeed once, when Sam Pothecary was standing at Taunton, Trueman felled him, as he passed, with a blow of his steel right toe-cap on the ankle so savage as to leave that mildest of umpires limping for a fortnight.

Now he had come to his full height, he hit the ground with the ball, in the constant manner of the Australian pace bowlers. Thus, in addition to his natural outswing – often late and from the line of the middle stump – which remained his deadliest weapon, especially on good pitches, he could make the most of a green wicket with some movement off the seam. He could also now bowl a highly disconcerting yorker, though not with the accuracy of his later years; and, of course, the bouncer occurred as frequent – too frequent – variation.

Such was the range of weapons the batsman faced in the moments before Trueman checked and went into his reaction routine. When an opponent edged him he registered an almost passionate blend of disgust and resentment against fate. If there was a scramble or a muddle, two agonised upraised hands expressed his – and reflected the spectators' – torment of suspense. If nothing happened, he would rock back on his heels with a word for the batsman, or the wicket-keeper, silly-mid off, the slips, short leg – or all of them – before he tossed back the shock of hair jerked over his forehead by the effort of delivery, gave a hoist to his concertina-ed trousers, tugged the wicket-keeper's return out of the air, and turned into his belligerent walk back, rolling the right shirt sleeve which was unfurled by every delivery of his life. It was a performance of drama, skill and character which held the attention as few bowlers have ever contrived outside the relatively short period of playing action.

The histrionics, the mighty oaths, the byplay, the talk, were elaborations – part of the Trueman spectacle but not of the bowling itself. They could even tend to obscure the fact that Fred Trueman now was a very fast bowler indeed. Batsmen knew it; those of limited ability with a degree of anxiety which delighted him. He could generally be relied upon to observe the code of the fast bowler's union, and refrain from bowling bumpers at its other members and, in fact, at non-batsmen in general. In return he expected – indeed, batted on the assumption of – similarly scrupulous non-violence from opposing bowlers. He had by now discovered and subsequently increased, the ability – which Ted MacDonald of Australia and Lancashire also possessed – of destroying a tail in little time. The best batsmen might still fancy themselves to take three or four runs an over from his vagaries; but even they could not be sure of surviving the best of his attack.

By thought and practice he had improved in the other

departments of the game: he was a capable fieldsman, either in the deep, where he returned low and accurately – to the surprise of some batsmen – with either hand (his father was left-handed); or close in, where his rapid reflexes helped him to some brilliant catches at short leg. Moreover, if he had no extensive range of strokes, he could, at Yorkshire's need and expectation, play safely with a straight bat in defence, drive with not quite so straight a bat, or pull through mid-wicket with marked, if crooked, power and pleasure.

At last he was the man he always felt himself to be; he recognised his suddenly increased speed and ability with delight but not surprise. Now he was unquestionably as threatening as he had always believed himself to be, dealing out a lethal bumper to chasten a disrespectful batsman – or simply one whose looks he did not like. Even so, he was going to surprise himself.

This was the first of a four-match Test series and one of some moment. All Yorkshire was deeply conscious, proud and – at hint of criticism – touchy – about the fact that Lord's had, for the first time, appointed a professional as captain of England and that the man chosen was Leonard Hutton, of Yorkshire, recognised there as the finest batsman in the world.

Certainly at this juncture, and for some years subsequently, Len Hutton understood Fred Trueman as a bowler – if not as a man – as well as anyone in the world. Ever since Trueman began to play for Yorkshire Hutton had been standing at mid-off, impressed by his potential speed, wincing at his prodigalities; observing all and, from time to time, offering comment or advice in a voice so quiet that Fred, in the constant heat of all his moments, often hardly heard. As a captain, Len Hutton was split-minded about Trueman. He himself had taken the brunt of that unnerving Australian fast attack of Miller and Lindwall when they could use the intimidating methods of their kind without fear of retaliation. He was for years the prime target of their attack, the man to be rid of for, once he was gone, the match was won. Therefore he relished, emotionally and, as captain, tactically, the thought of a counter weapon that might cancel out the long uncontested Australian advantage.

He did not retain the post of captain long enough to deploy Trueman at his finest; perhaps, in some ways, that was his chief regret, for he knew that his best was yet to come. When everyone else – critics and public, at least – hailed Trueman for his feats in 1952, Len Hutton said – not aloud and not for publication – that he thought the young man immature, in some ways fortunate, in some unfortunate, to have come upon such success so early and – in polite confidence – so easily. 'He is not ready,' he said, 'not nearly ready and next year when the Australians come, everyone else will realise it; he is fast: but he is not a Test Match bowler against Australian batsmen because he cannot bowl as he knows he ought to bowl. Unless he has bad luck, he is going to be a very good fast bowler; but not yet; not for five or six years.' Even as late as 1956, after he had left the captaincy of England Hutton could look back dispassionately at the scene and say 'The best of Fred Trueman is still to come – in two or three years, I think'. With the benefit of hindsight it can be seen that Hutton was right.

As a captain he always asked the highest pace – but controlled pace – from his fast bowlers; and to ensure he had it, he was prepared, if necessary, to bowl them in short spells. He believed that reduction of pace was weakness; that the greatest speed was more effective than anything else, and to wield this optimum weapon he would go to almost any lengths. Thus, in Australia in 1954-5, he nursed Tyson and Statham with extreme care so that, if he threw them into bowl themselves out to win a match – as he twice did – they could and would do so. Then, afterwards, he did not hesitate to tell them to go away from cricket, to the beach for a week or more, and come back recharged.

Thus he used Truman in 1952. He knew him to be strong and, while he doubted his stamina and control, he recognised that his speed could destroy Indian batsmen with their known dislike of fast bowling. Against any other attack they might plod to huge totals, but he knew them to be inexperienced against pace which the placid nature of Indian wickets has discouraged to the point of extinction in their domestic game.

Hazare won the toss and India batted on a typical Headingley pitch of amiable batting pace; the ball ran away quickly over the closely mown outfield and bowlers could expect to labour. Trueman's opening spell showed no profit against Roy and Gaekwad and Hutton took him off quickly, only to bring him back, when Gaekwad was out, to bowl at Umrigar, a consistently heavy scorer against medium-paced and spin bowling, but known to be vulnerable to pace. Surely enough, he fenced at Trueman and gave him his first Test wicket, an edged catch to Evans. A major stand, of 222, between the young Manjrekar – who took many runs by back foot strokes off Trueman in a capable 133 – and Hazare, brought India to 264 for three, the brink of the large total the wicket had promised and which, in doubtful weather, might set them in a winning position. Then Hutton, characteristically provident, had Bedser and Trueman adequately rested not merely to weather the last hour but to contest it. Hazare was caught at the wicket off Bedser and, before another run was scored, Trueman had Manjrekar well taken by Watkins, low at second slip and, two balls afterwards, bowled Gopinath off the edge of a hasty stroke. In less than ten minutes the whole shape of the game had been altered and India ended the day 272 for six. Next morning, after overnight rain had made the pitch difficult, Laker mopped up the innings. Trueman's three wickets for 89 in twenty-six overs was as much as anyone close to him – except Trueman himself – had expected of him in these conditions. He had accounted for numbers three, five and seven in the batting order. By a captain's standards, though, he had bought his wickets; Bedser bowled thirty-three overs for 38 runs (two wickets), Laker twenty-two for 39 runs (four wickets): while the 89 off Trueman came from only twenty-six overs: even the leg spinner, Jenkins, was more economical with 78 from twenty-seven overs.

While Phadkar, Ramchand and Hazare kept the game tight with medium pace, the off-spinner Ghulam Ahmad bowled skilfully, Graveney, Watkins and Jenkins grafted and Evans struck a bouncy 66 to give England a lead of 41 which, since they would have to take fourth innings, the experts doubted was enough to give them a strong chance of winning.

The noblest stage for a Yorkshire cricketer is the Headingley Test – the most important occasion of the county's cricketing calendar. The great day of the match is the Saturday, when the faithful make their pilgrimage from all the Ridings and the ground is full; and the high peak of Saturday is mid-afternoon, when all the dense crowd is settled, and outside there is the maximum radio and television audience. Such was the setting for Fred Trueman in 1952 when India began their second innings with a fair prospect of beating England. Accused of having written the script for it himself he said, 'Ay, and I made myself principal boy'.

The atmosphere of that afternoon remains unforgettable. The first time the Saturday crowd saw Len Hutton was when he led out the players through the usual Headingley corridor of small boys, and all Yorkshire recognised and shared his distinction in the long, deep and warm applause that greeted him. There was a separate, if less impressive, salute for the county's other representative who, as his captain set the field, made his way in a semi-casual, semi-dramatic way to the stumps at the Kirkstall Lane end – which gave him a downhill run-in – paced out a twenty-two yard run and, deeply immersed in the crowd's interest, took the loosening trial run-up which was then established Yorkshire practice.

It was five minutes to three: everyone inside the packed ground settled down: they are more meticulous about this at Headingley than on most English grounds: and if a Yorkshire-man is involved – as happened especially when Hutton or Sut-

cliffe was opening a Test innings – all attention is centred on
him.

The pitch, easy on the first day, difficult on the second morning, was helpful to spin until the end: now it was lively but, on
the whole, honest: only one ball from a pace bowler did anything remarkable.

Trueman's first ball to Pankaj Roy, well outside the line of
the off stump, was allowed to go through to the wicket-keeper.
The second was a bumper; Roy moved inside it and tried to
hook, was not quick enough and skied it off the top edge; a
hush while it was in the air and as it dropped for Compton to
catch it at second slip, a roar of triumph and, growing out of
it, congratulations for their own man: none for one wicket. In
the next over Alec Bedser bowled the one ball of the day that
behaved unpredictably; it lifted off a length to the left-handed
Gaekwad who could not avoid it, took the shoulder of the bat
and was caught by Laker in the gully: up went another immense shout: none for two wickets.

At the fall of the first wicket Hazare sent in Mantri, the
wicket-keeper, a dogged, defensive bat who had been not out in
the first innings. Trueman, stimulated by the tension, swaggered
back to his mark, raced up his curving run and let loose a near
half-volley which knocked Mantri's off stump out of the ground :
up went the hunting call that a cricket crowd keeps pent up, and
lets out almost before the event when its own team is on the
kill: none for three wickets.

Manjrekar, top scorer of the first innings, was a neat, cool
man, after Hazare as good a player of pace bowling as any
Indian batsman of the period; he had been hard on Trueman
in scoring his earlier century. The silence was hardly credible
in the presence of over 30,000 people. The atmosphere would
have affected older and more hardened men than Trueman but
he held himself in admirable balance, bowled another straight
ball of full length, Manjrekar, surprisingly enough, aimed a
cover drive, was hopelessly late; again the off stump was torn

out; the killer cry went up with increased intensity and the score was none for four wickets – all in fourteen balls.

After the pandemonium, the crowd fell momentarily still, as if in disbelief before a deep, excited babble of talk broke out all round the ground. Hazare, a lean, steady-eyed, resolute, military-looking man – he was an officer in the army of the Gaekwar of Baroda – came in himself. Trueman was 'on' a hat-trick and Hutton summoned up a close field of eight men behind the bat. Trueman gathered himself: in a prickling silence he swept up once more and tried to bowl a yorker. Hazare moved into line, bat close to pad: the ball passed an inch wide of the outside edge – and of the off stump: the crowd let out its breath in a huge, collective sigh.

In suitable conditions Fred Trueman could, and often did, swing the ball sharply – if not quite so prodigiously as he sometimes claimed – but one who was looking directly down their line can state categorically that the three balls which put out Roy, Mantri and Manjrekar at Headingley in 1952 were all completely straight – and extremely fast.

None for four wickets had never been seen on a Test Match scoreboard before. Indeed, one evening newspaper office telephoned its correspondent to confirm that the figure had been given the wrong way round and that India were, in fact, 4 for no wicket – and received the insistence on nought for four incredulously. Statistics apart, Trueman had wrecked India's strong position. Understandably over-eager, he tried too hard, bowled an occasional loose ball and was taken off after four overs while, in a spell immediately after tea, he could not break the stand between Hazare and Phadkar through which India strove to recover. Ten minutes from the end of the day Hutton, with his shrewd tactical sense, brought him back and Trueman, to his extravagant jubilation, clean bowled Hazare – again by straightness and immense pace. That was the decisive blow: Hutton did not need him the next day when Jenkins and Bedser finished off the Indian innings and England, without hurry, won by seven wickets.

Here, at last, was an English fast-bowler who by a spectacular performance had turned a Test Match; he was good headlines; gossip, stories – true and false – followed; he was good-looking in a rugged way – virile, anyway – Yorkshire (which means sharing the true 'mystique' of cricket) and a 'character' – so everyone said. Who could or should be surprised that he revelled in all this attention? After all, it merely confirmed what he had known all the time, while the Yorkshire committee had been too dim to see it; and if he did not carry off the situation with the poise of an experienced public figure, who can blame him?

Ten days later he was released from an RAF tour of Holland and Germany to play in the second Test at Lord's. He arrived at the team's hotel tired after the journey. Len Hutton arranged for him to sleep long and be called late to ensure that he had adequate rest even in advance of net practice on the day before the match.

This was the match in which Vinoo Mankad, released by his league club to play for India, scored 72 and 184, bowled ninety-seven overs and took five first innings wickets, but still could not prevent England winning by eight wickets.

It demonstrated clearly the merits and demerits of Fred Trueman as a bowler at that time. On a good batting wicket he discharged his prime duty by taking wickets – eight in all – numbers one, three, eight and nine in the first innings; three, seven, eight and ten in the second (quickly brought on for the purpose by Len Hutton, he disposed of the 'apprehensive' Polly Umrigar each time). On the other hand, his fifty-two overs cost 182 runs and he was an embarrassment to Hutton on tactical grounds. At the beginning of the match – India again won the toss and batted first – Mankad took risks to force the pace and, precisely when Hutton wanted to tie him down and fray his patience until he played an injudicious stroke, Trueman, by bowling short, gave him constant opportunities to cut or hook.

This was then Trueman's weakness; on a plumb wicket the good batsman could invariably find one or two hittable balls in every over. On this occasion, too, Mankad's onslaught on Roley Jenkins – he not only hit him off, but out of Test cricket for ever – meant that Trueman could not be nursed. He had to be used in longer spells than at Headingley, and became loose and expensive. Hutton counselled and cautioned but the runs still came; fortunately for Trueman wickets came as well. In the first innings he ultimately took the wicket of Mankad – brilliantly caught by Watkins at leg slip – but not until he had made 72 out of a total of 235 in which only one other batsman made more than 35. When conditions favour batting it is not unreasonable to buy wickets – but only by design. When India batted again and Hazare joined Mankad in the stand that might have tilted the game, Mankad took 13 runs from the first five balls of a Trueman over and Hazare four off the last. Test captains cannot afford such prodigality. Eight for 182 is not by any means an unhappy return for a fast bowler on a batsman's pitch. Yet, it serves to emphasize that Trueman's figures in the other three Tests of this series – twenty-one wickets for 204, giving an average of under ten – could not have been achieved against good batsmen on good wickets. Some might argue that they could not be achieved against good batsmen anywhere nor against any batsman on good wickets. Still, cricketers are entitled to their share of luck; Trueman's was not always good and it was no bad thing that this fortune should have come when, and as spectacularly, as it did.

An immaculate innings of 150 by Hutton – disciplined, poised and punctuated by cover drives of mellow perfection – and a gay, headlong 104 by Godfrey Evans gave England an advantage they never lost; and although Mankad and his fellow fingerspinner, Ghulam Ahmad, fought the issue down to the end, India were beaten by eight wickets.

Trueman played against the tourists in the match following the Test – this time for the Combined Services. There was no one there of sufficient authority to impose any strict control on the elated young man who was being hailed in headlines as the irresistible fast bowler. The idea of his speed went to his head; he bowled long hops all over the place. After being hit for 46 runs in fourteen overs, he fell in a deeply dug foot-hole and was carried off the field with an ankle so seriously injured that he was not fit to play again until the third Test – at Old Trafford.

There, again, circumstances combined against the Indians and in favour of Trueman. This time England won the toss and their first innings, frequently interrupted by bad light and rain, lasted until Hutton, who made another highly accomplished century, declared at 347 for nine on Saturday morning. By then the pitch was wet through, and although no Indian bowler was fast enough to exploit it, Trueman found it much to his liking.

Bowling from the Stretford end with a strong wind blowing in over his right shoulder, he brought the ball off the pitch at immense speed, making it rear intimidatingly – and the Indians *were* intimidated. With unusual and impressive good sense, he used the bouncer only as what he called 'a reminder' and said, humbly enough, 'I only had to bowl straight to get wickets'. Hutton set a close field of three slips, three gullies, a silly point and two short legs and Trueman bowled to it. It was a stirring spectacle, the mounting run up and then, as the square-on position of the approach gave way to the side-ways-on of delivery, the poised left side, arm towering high, came over like the prow of a sailing ship riding a wave. The actor sensed, and held, his audience. Every time the ball was edged or lifted it went to hand and, in a glorious display of fielding, everything catchable was caught. It was cricket of the dramatic intensity which only concentrated attack – but not batting – can create.

Bedser opened the bowling: Mankad drove his first ball through the covers for four and glanced the last of the over for Lock to launch himself forward at short leg and make the catch: it was the first time he had touched the ball in a Test Match. Trueman in his opening, four-over spell had Roy, Adhikari – one of the few members of the Indian side to face him resolutely – and Phadkar – off a fully struck slash – caught. Then came Umrigar who at one point retreated so far that Lock, at backward short-leg, said "I say, Polly, do you mind going back, I can't see the bowler when you stand there': when Trueman bowled him, India were 17 for five. Hazare and Manjrekar devotedly put on 28 before, soon after lunch, Bedser bowled the Indian captain while Trueman, with the cruellest ball of the match, which fired up too fast to be avoided, had Manjrekar caught at short leg. He swept away Divecha – convulsively bowled – Ramchand and Sen in a couple of overs; and, when India were out for 58, his figures for the innings were 8.4 overs: two maidens: 31 runs: eight wickets Those who announce such records pointed out that this was the finest analysis ever returned by a truly fast bowler in a Test. Statistics apart, nothing was more significant about his bowling than its accuracy: almost all the runs scored off him came from snicks which pierced the intensively manned close field to the uncovered boundaries.

He began the second innings by inflicting a 'duck' on Pankaj Roy for the third time in consecutive Test innings and hitting Adhikari so violently in the mouth with a fiery lifter that he had to be carried off. Then, when he was in terrific fettle, he had an attack of 'stitch'. Although Adhikari returned to make top score of the innings, Bedser and Lock took the remaining wickets and by half past five India, with a second innings total of 82, had become only the second team to be bowled out twice in a single day's play of a Test Match.

Trueman's pleasure at match figures of nine for 40 in 16.4 overs was slightly dimmed – though he made the utmost of its humour, irony and superficial injustice – by a telegram from his commanding officer – surely a cricket enthusiast with a mischievous sense of humour – which read 'Report back to unit

8am Sunday'. He had, he observed with mock dolefulness, bowled himself out of three days' leave.

Released again for the 'Roses' match, he continued his run of success when, on a drying pitch at Old Trafford, he and Eric Burgin – a medium pace inswing bowler who had been in the Sheffield United team with him – bowled out Lancashire in their first innings for 65. Trueman took five for 26; and, called back with the new ball at the end when Yorkshire were pressing for a win, he took two of the three wickets they needed: but the Lancashire last pair, Frank Parr and Bob Berry, held on for a draw.

So to the fourth and last Test, at the Oval, in more uncertain weather. England batted through the first day and until lunchtime on the second when a thunderstorm stopped play and Hutton declared, leaving the Indians to wait, in justifiable trepidation, for another offensive by Bedser and Trueman. Bedser bowled a maiden over, which included a sharp rap on the knuckles for Mankad from a ball that lifted off a length. Hutton set an arc of five slips and two men at short leg and Trueman, in the tense atmosphere he had come to enjoy, tore up to the persevering but hapless Pankaj Roy and dropped the first ball short. It reared up, Roy fended it off his ribs with his bat and Lock made the catch an inch or two above the ground at short leg. The success went to Trueman's head as it had not done at Manchester: the remaining five balls of the over were all bouncers which Adhikari was able to watch past without playing a stroke. In Bedser's second over Mankad scored a two and a three before Adhikari pushed down on an inswinger and Trueman, in the leg trap, dived forward and scooped it up. Next he sent down a bumper to Mankad who tried to hook, mishit, and sent up such a steep skier that Evans could stroll round behind the slips to catch it. Off the next ball Manjrekar was dropped at slip but in his next over Bedser, who wisely kept the ball up to the bat, had him caught at short leg; and then yorked Umrigar: the Indian score was 6 for five wickets. Hazare and Phadkar lasted the rest of the day, to 49 for five and there was no play on Saturday. In a single over on Monday morning Trueman was no balled three times for dragging and took both their wickets, and when he bowled Sen to end the innings at 98 he had an analysis of five for 48 from sixteen overs. Hutton, pressing to win all four Tests of his first captaincy, invited India to follow on but, before they could do so and mercifully for their shattered batsmen, the rain returned and washed away the rest of the match.

Fred Trueman with twenty-nine wickets had set a new record for an English bowler in a series with India. He was top of the Yorkshire averages with thirty-two wickets at 14 and second to Roly Thompson (who had only eighteen wickets) in the national table with sixty-one at 13.78: and if he conceded roughly three runs an over, he had the amazing striking-rate, which even he never again approached over a full season, of a wicket every 4.7 overs.

Out of the 1952 summer, too, came the first of the classic Trueman stories and the one he has been at most pains to deny. It was related that, at a dinner given by the Indian High Commissioner in London to the Indian and English teams, Fred, as the outstanding success of the series, was placed at the top table. He sat next to a high dignitary of the Indian government who was deeply engaged in conversation with his neighbour on the other side when Fred, unable otherwise to attracted his attention, gave him a nudge in the ribs and said 'Hey, Gunga Din, pass t'salt'. Fred has sworn that this story is completely fictitious and that he was never in a position to have said anything of the kind. It is, though, part of the Trueman legend. All his protests cannot expunge it from the minds of the millions of people throughout the cricketing countries of the world who have never met him but who have repeated that story until it became more true than much of the truth in his image.

Len Hutton, interviewed after the Oval Test, gave it as his

Everton Weekes bowled by Trueman, Edgbaston 1957

'In his pomp'

opinion that Trueman who was as yet 'a little on the colt side' would eventually be as fine a fast bowler as Lindwall. Fred, for his part, was content. He had proved himself the fast bowler he had always known he was. He had reason to be more than ordinarily pleased for, although he later became a far greater bowler when he was in 1952, he never again had such a high proportion of outstanding analyses. He gave up playing football which might endanger his fitness: that winter he was selected by the Cricket Writers' Club as the Outstanding Young Cricketer of the Year: and in the following spring he became one of *Wisden's* 'Five Cricketers of the Year'. He was not surprised.

Once more, as happened often in the life of F. S. Trueman, a phase ended with such absolute finality that it might have been the end of a story. Certainly it was never the same again.

E

CHAPTER SIX
A Day in the Sun

If Fred Trueman's bowling figures of 1952 did him something more generous than justice, those of 1953 did him something less: if the weather of the earlier year helped him by producing wet, lively wickets, that of 1953 gave him wet, dead ones. Yorkshire deteriorated in effectiveness and from second position in the Championship to joint twelfth – probably the worst season of their history. Trueman, who had begun the season of 1952 so magnificently as to make his inclusion in the Test team certain, was now unable to produce either figures or form to justify his selection. If August brought him a happier ending, it was a patch of brightness in an otherwise frustrating period of his career; and little better was to follow it for some time.

The England team Len Hutton had envisaged was approaching maturity. A cadre rather than an eleven, it had widely variant bowling strengths. Either Lock or Wardle was the slow left arm bowler; for some years neither was ever chosen for the Lord's Test where England went in with an extra seam bowler. The pace bowling also was not permanent. Trueman, Statham and, within a year, Tyson, were of true pace, with the slightly slower Moss and Loader in reserve. Still, however, Bedser, the complete stock-and-shock fast-medium bowler, was an automatic choice for a decade and Bailey, a genuine all-rounder, often took the second seam bowler's place so that another batsman could be brought in. Thus selection could be made a matter of tactical alternatives for specific conditions.

Len Hutton remained torn between the economical, fast-medium precision of Bedser, Bailey and spin of Lock, Tattersall, Laker and Wardle on the one hand; and, on the other, the as yet immature pace of Trueman – fast enough to be disturbing but often erratic – and Statham who was accurate but had not yet reached his full speed.

The time had not yet come when Hutton was happy to go into a Test Match with two absolutely fast bowlers. Three times in the series he opened with Bedser and Bailey and, until the last match, England subsisted on only three specialist bowlers. Trueman and Statham each played in one Test; each was once the player left out of the twelve summoned to a match; and it was announced that Statham – who had played at Lord's – was not sufficiently fit to have been considered for Old Trafford, when Trueman was called up and omitted.

Trueman, unable to play a complete season, had much to do to win the only fast bowling place from Statham who had a full and successful summer – 101 wickets at 16.33 by comparison with Trueman's forty-four at 32.06.

He did not play for Yorkshire until his service leave began towards the end of May. Then his first cricket, after ten days immobilised with an ankle injury, was the Roses match. He was sick and unable to eat all day and had a recurrence of stitch in the afternoon. Nevertheless, for some weeks later he would have been grateful for such a return as his three wickets – all good ones – in Lancashire's first innings. For, after that only four of the five Cambridge University batsmen to be put out relieved a depressing period when in a series of five unfinished matches, he took only seven wickets. He missed both Yorkshire's fixtures with the Australians; whom he watched as twelfth man in the Old Trafford Test and the reporters travelling with the touring side made a point of going to Old Trafford to see him bowl against Lancashire. There seemed, though, no prospect of closer contact between him and the touring team as he ploughed through a weary, wet summer, developing the savage hatred of slow pitches which subsequently provided the theme for some of his most volcanic invective. Apart from match figures of eight for 120 in a two-day fixture between the RAF and 'A Pakistani XI' – which proved nothing – and four for 93 for Yorkshire against Surrey, the selectors who, one sensed, wanted to pick him, had no shred of current evidence to justify it. At the end of July they applied to the Air Ministry for his release so that they could watch him again and, for Yorkshire against Kent, at Scarborough, in encouraging conditions for pace bowling, he suddenly produced one of the old, fierce bursts. He took the wickets of numbers one to four in the first innings; made the initial break through and finished with six for 47 in the second. That performance produced the instant result – while the match was still in progress – of his being named among the first ten chosen for the coming winter tour of the West Indies. A valuable six for 109 in Lancashire's 373 at Bramall Lane; a loose spell followed by a burst of three for 23 in a six runs defeat by Leicestershire; and he was one of the twelve players summoned to the last Test, at the Oval when, after four drawn matches, The Ashes were at issue.

This amounted virtually to inclusion in the eleven, since the twelve included Lock – whose fitness was not certain – and Wardle who presumably was his standby. So it proved: Lock was fit, Wardle became twelfth man and, by comparison with the team for the fourth Test, Watson – desperately unfortunate after the innings with which he had saved the Lord's Test – and Simpson, were left out for May and Trueman – a shift of England's team balance in that, for the first time in the series, a fourth specialist bowler replaced a specialist batsman.

Hutton lost the toss for the fifth time in the series, Australia batted and Bedser bowled the first over to Hassett. Nothing could have been more sharply indicative of the feeling in England about English fast bowlers in general and Trueman in particular than the cheers that broke out all round the ground when Hutton called him up to bowl from the pavilion end.

The pitch was relatively easy in pace – those at The Oval

generally favoured spin at this period – and the air was wind-less and sultry, sapping for fast bowlers. Nothing quenched Trueman: he was back where he believed he had the right to be, and he was not to be put down. Hassett pushed his first ball to leg for a single and then – perhaps the most signi-ficant facet of English cricket feeling of the period – when his second ball was a bouncer to Morris, the cheering broke out all over again; thus deep were the wounds Miller and Lindwall had inflicted on the body of English cricket.

Trueman made a half-convinced – and therefore unconvinc-ing – appeal for a catch at the wicket from his fifth ball and it was refused : but off the sixth, Morris's hard leg glance was dropped by Compton at leg slip. He twice deceived Morris to the point of hasty correction with his slower ball but, after five overs thrifty enough to cost only twelve runs, he went off for Bailey.

His next spell, of only three overs, cost 21 runs; his last ball before lunch was a bouncer which passed over Hassett's bent neck. Meanwhile Bedser and Bailey had accounted for Morris and Miller.

A shower lengthened the luncheon interval by five minutes and put sufficient life into the pitch to grant both Bedser and Trueman invigorating life and lift. Hassett was caught at short leg off Bedser. Then Trueman, telling his captain what he intended to do, and predicting the outcome, dealt a bouncer to that habitual hooker, Harvey, who wheeled on it, hooked too late, and Hutton made the catch running away from mid-wicket with his back to the batsman. The time of a short shower afterwards, de Courcy hung out his bat to a lifter, Evans took the catch and Archer came in to face Trueman with an arc of six men in the slips. Six slips for an Australian batsman facing an English bowler – the crowd laughed its delight. True-man's figures for a five-over spell were two for 21 when Hutton sent him into the deep to re-charge.

Twenty minutes afterwards he was back and, for all the

pressure of the sticky heat, there was a cocky spring in his run as he came up. He bowled an outswinger of full length, a little outside the line of the off stump; Hole aimed a free cover drive at it; again Evans took the catch. Trueman, three for 23 since lunch, had brought Australia to the sore straits of 160 for six, when he took his sweater again.

Lindwall, with first Davidson and then Langley, led the innings clear of disaster and at twenty-to-six Hutton called back a wilted-looking Trueman, his sweat-soaked shirt sticking to his bowed back. Almost at once he had Johnston dropped at slip and then Lindwall, Australia's top scorer with 62, edged a lifter and Evans caught the third of Trueman's four wickets in the day. His four for 86 was the best analysis among the England bowlers.

On Tuesday morning he contributed ten of the 69 runs by which the last three wickets created a valuable England lead of 31. Hutton gave him only two overs – which cost four runs – at the start of the second Australian innings and did not need him again. He took two close catches as Laker and Lock, with nine wickets between them – de Courcy was run out – put out Australia for 162. So England won the match by eight wickets, took the series, and regained The Ashes after nineteen years. At the end an emotional crowd streamed across the ground calling for the players. Trueman and his teammates stood in the brightest sunshine any English cricket player can know.

Before the Test he had helped the RAF to beat the Royal Navy by taking ten wickets in the match at Lord's: after it, he did almost as much against The Army with his best figures for the RAF, five for 16 in the first innings, two for 16 in the second: Peter Sainsbury and Rupert Robinson saved the game for the Army with only three wickets left.

His only appearance of the season for the Combined Services was against the Australians at the Kingston Festival in September. When he arrived he found that his usual captain, Alan Shirreff – also of the RAF – was playing under Mike Ains-

worth of the Navy; and that Jim Pressdee, a fellow aircrafts-
man, had been left out in favour of a sailor. His indignation was
even greater when he, England's opening bowler in the final
Test Match was not given the first over, which went – together
with choice of ends – to Terry Spencer. Then his usual – and
specialist – position of short leg was given to an army officer;
the final fuel was added to his indignation when, after three
wickets had gone cheaply, that same army officer dropped
Keith Miller off him – at short leg, of course. He could not
then know that Miller would score 262 not out – the highest
score of his career – nor that de Courcy would make 204 and
that the Australians would declare at 592 for four and win by
an innings. He was already, however, as he recalls, 'not interested in bowling'; and at one point he was missed in the field
and discovered sitting on the sight screen, smiling broadly.

The pitch was good, de Courcy was in form; Trueman
bowled bouncers at him and de Courcy, who was a very good
hooker, hooked him hard. Trueman's 14 over were hit for 95
runs; non-bowlers took over and, after reports to authority, he
was informed that he would never be asked to play for the
Combined Services again. The notification arrived, to his mirth,
two days after he was demobilised.

He appeared no more that season for Yorkshire, for whom
his record was 38 wickets at 28.38 : Foord, statistically more
successful, with 62 at 25.83, nevertheless now decided finally
to devote himself to school-teaching.

Trueman played in a one-day fixture at Ealing for the RAF
Fund, was demobilised on 16 September, and went back home
to Maltby. There the people of the town had so heavily over-
subscribed the collection fund to present an illuminated address
to its most distinguished cricketing offspring that the Chairman
of the Maltby Urban District Council was able to hand him
a new and suitably lettered cricket bag purchased from the
surplus. It would serve him admirably on his imminent tour of
the West Indies under Len Hutton.

CHAPTER SEVEN

The Clouded Prospect

Life had never seemed more promising for Fred Trueman than on the morning of 12 December, 1953 when he went to London Airport to join the first MCC team to fly out on a tour, and the first captained by a professional – Leonard Hutton. The pit and National Service were behind him; he had his Yorkshire cap; he had made an appreciable contribution to England's most important Test win since the second World War. He was young, single, fit, mettlesome, with no real responsibilities and, in the most envied aspect of the cricketer's life, he was going to fly out from the English winter to the sunshine of the West Indies.

Irritations began for him from the start of the tour. The team's aeroplane developed an engine fault and, instead of taking its tropical suited passengers to Bermuda as intended, it was diverted to Gander under heavy snow and in twenty-eight degrees of frost. They went to Bermuda for a ten-day stay and some practice matches at the request and – high – expense of the island cricketers. Trueman found immense difficulty in bowling because of the painful impact of his left foot on the concrete base over which the matting wicket was stretched. To overcome the difficulty he ran wide of the strip which impaired his direction, and in the effort to correct it, he broke the rhythm of his run-up. Len Hutton, too, was unfortunate; he was caught at the wicket off the first ball of the tour – bowled by a man named Mulder who thus staked his only known claim to cricketing immortality.

Much that was to happen in Trueman's subsequent career might be attributed – he himself would certainly attribute it – to his strained relations with Len Hutton on this trip. It is easy to see how the two would antagonise one another. Trueman was young, feeling his oats, glorying in the violence of being a fast bowler, quick-tempered, and apt to make the wrong joke out of sheer excitement. It was, too, his first overseas tour and he did not know the form. He has always regarded himself proudly as bluntly-spoken Yorkshireman and at this time he was even less diplomatic than he became later. He sensed, and resented, the attitude of the elder players who knew the touring ropes, were more self-contained and had little interest in the younger man. He was quick to see nepotism in the fact that, when a batting place became open for the Barbados Test, it was given to Charles Palmer, an amateur and the team-manager, instead of to Ken Suttle who had just scored 96 and 62 on the same ground in the colony match. He did not hesitate to voice his opinion on this and his other grievances and, if he did not utter his thoughts on some unfavourable courses of events on the field, his gestures and expressions left no possible doubt of them. Len Hutton, then as always, was quiet, withdrawn; he found rowdiness or any form of horseplay distasteful. He was, moreover, deeply concerned for his captaincy. No one was more uncomfortably aware than he that a considerable body of opinion in the cricket establishment had been opposed to the concept of a professional as captain of England; and that any indication of inability to discharge the diplomatic or disciplinary side of his duties could be taken as indicating the unsuitability of a paid player for the post. When they played for Yorkshire, he and Trueman were both capped professionals and, despite his seniority, he was simply 'Len' to the younger man. Now it had to be 'skipper' – had to be because the issue was delicate and the balance of the captaincy so inherently precarious. Hutton did not doubt his own practical ability; the quality of his batting and his knowledge of strategy could not be questioned; but this precise issue, of his ability to command the outer trappings of respect from a young and fettled player, was the very essence of his problem. The need for the formality was pointed out to Trueman, who simply thought it stupid: after all, they were still the same two men who had played for Yorkshire on Christian name terms in the previous summer, and who would do so again next summer. Eventually he accepted the ruling, but without conviction or pleasure. He would remember 'skipper' dutifully enough in peaceful moments but, when he was taken off or given an instruction he did not relish it was 'Nay, nay, Len'; and that became an irritant to both of them.

Hutton himself was immensely sensitive to atmosphere and to public relations. He saw that Trueman's approach – which he commended as his 'fast bowler's temper' – was likely to arouse strong reactions among West Indians. On the other hand he was deeply concerned to win the Test series and while conscious of Trueman's potential he was also aware that he could be easily cast down, when he would lose heart for bowling, so he sought to nurse him by not being over-strict and by allowing him his high spirits.

Moreover Charles Palmer, the tour manager, the most charming of men, was easy-going, certainly not a disciplinarian and if a strong line had to be taken with a player, it was obviously Hutton who would have to take it. By these two baffling, contradictory attitudes – the preservation of his dignity and reluctance to clamp down on Trueman, Hutton soured the relationship between them. Hutton believed his players could foster a combative attitude towards the Tests if they refused to fraternise with the other side. Again the gregarious Trueman was infuriated.

It is usual in touring sides for players to pair up, especially when, as often happens, they have to share accommodation, and Trueman 'roomed' with Tony Lock. In human terms it was a happy arrangement: and it remained Fred Trueman's deepest

and most enduring friendship in cricket. They were both extro-
verted; both deeply committed cricketers: both passionately
demonstrative in their responses to cricket event – an appeal, a
dropped catch or a luckily edged stroke – and both talked
cricket incessantly off the field. Both needed constantly to be
reassured of their merits and they reassured one another: over
their years in the England team, too, they picked up some
superb catches off one another's bowling. They were later to
realise that on this tour their association could be a disadvantage. They were both young, both touring for the first time,
gauche, unfamiliar with protocol, both quick to anger, both
forthright in stating their views: these were dangerous tenden-
cies in their position: but the idea of danger did not occur to
them.

Trueman's first ball of the West Indies tour proper – against
the Combined Parishes in Jamaica – was edged by Michael
Frederick to second slip, where Alan Moss – who should never
have been there – dropped it. Frederick, who had previously
played for Derbyshire, went on to score 84 and was chosen for
the first Test.

George Headley, the greatest player in the history of Jamaican
cricket, and idolised by the island population, also played in
the Parishes match. He was now rising forty-five – by West
Indian standards, old for Test cricket – and for some years he
had lived in England, playing as a professional in the Birmingham League. He had appeared in one Test of the home
series with England in 1947-8 and one on the tour of India in
1948-9; his scores were 29, 7 not out and 2; and it had been
generally assumed that his first-class career was ended. The
people of Jamaica did not share that view; they raised over
£1,000 by public subscription to bring George Headley back to
the West Indies so that he could play in this Test series, and it
was a matter of Caribbean political certainty that he would play
in at least the Jamaica Test.

He captained the Parishes team and in the first innings was

caught at short leg off Moss for one: when he came in the second time Trueman bowled him a bouncer and was both surprised and annoyed when Headley, always a strong back-foot player, hooked it out of the ground. A couple of overs afterwards Trueman tried him with another bouncer; Headley again tried to hook, missed and the ball broke a bone in his arm. The crowd erupted in anger; Trueman had to be given a police escort from the ground and, for the rest of the stay in Jamaica, he was 'Mr Bumper Man'. The injury kept Headley out of the first colony match at Sabina Park; in the second Trueman bowled him a sequence of good length balls, then put in the bouncer, Headley hooked it high, Suttle caught it on the run at long leg and he was out for five. Fortunately or unfortunately for him he made 53 not out in the second innings. He was twice missed and took four hours to make his runs; on the other hand, his stand with Holt probably saved Jamaica from defeat and, such was the strength of local feeling, that one of the island newspapers went so far as to say that he 'had hardly played a greater innings than this'. There were, too, threats to boycott the match and to dig up the pitch if Headley was not picked and when Frank Worrell reported unfit the West Indian selectors, with some relief, brought him in.

Trueman had still not recovered the smoothness of his run that had been lost on the concrete strip in Bermuda and since both Moss and Statham had bowled more accurately and effectively, his Test place was doubtful until he took five for 45 in the second innings, when he and Statham effectively won the first Jamaica match.

In this spell he bowled really fast and well. He still used the bumper too often, especially against West Indian batsmen who, on their own true wickets, are invariably strong hookers. He seemed almost to welcome and provoke the hostile reaction of the crowds to the short pitched ball that flew past the bats-man's head. Already a local song-writer singer had featured the number – to the tune of *What Shall We Do with a Drunken Sailor*

> What shall we do with Freddie Trueman?
> What shall we do with Freddie Trueman?
> Now he's bowling bumpers.
>> Head down and up she rises
>> Head down and up she rises
>> Head down and up she rises
>> He's a-bowling bumpers
> Four hundred on the scoreboard rises
> Four hundred on the scoreboard rises
> And still he's bowling bumpers.

Hutton, characteristically, decided to rely on pace and, leaving out Laker, played Statham, Moss, Trueman and Bailey. A typically shiny, bare Sabina Park wicket gave bowlers neither help nor encouragement. Trueman again had trouble with his run but he concentrated on bowling a length – sixteen overs for 32 runs – as West Indies made a slow start with 168 for two on the first day.

It had been agreed at an England team meeting that, as a tribute to George Headley's eminence, he would be given 'one off the mark' – the courtesy usually extended to a cricketer only in his benefit match. When he came in on the second morning, the fieldsmen moved deep, Statham bowled to him at no more than medium pace, he pushed to the leg side and, as he strolled the easy single, he raised his cap. Nevertheless, as he walked off the field, not out at tea, he surprised Trueman with the remark 'This isn't cricket any more, this is war'. He had lost his relish for the bouncer. Weekes had not: he hooked one from Trueman so hard that when it hit the concrete wall of the scoreboard it rebounded more than a pitch-length back on to the field. Headley made 16 in an hour before he swept and was caught by Graveney at short leg.

West Indies were 331 for six after tea next day when Hutton took the new ball and gave it to Trueman and Statham, who went through a savagely frustrating experience; in three-quarters-of-an-hour Gomez and McWatt put on 60 runs, almost all off the edge, and McWatt was dropped five times – three times off Trueman. That partnership tilted the match decisively. The English players were puzzled when, while Moss was bowling, some of the spectators began shouting 'We want Trueman': he had not hitherto been noticeably popular. They understood when a huge cheer went up as the scoreboard ticked up the 100 on his bowling analysis. It had been 96 and the crowd – or those who had wagered on it – wanted him to get his 'century' before the close of play. By the end of that second day he had bowled 32 overs for exactly 100 runs and no wickets: West Indies were 408 for seven. Next morning he took the tail-end wickets of Ramadhin and Valentine, but it had been a chastening experience. The crowd demonstrated against Jeffrey Stollmeyer, the West Indian captain, when, instead of enforcing the follow-on, he decided to bat again 247 ahead. Trueman opened the bowling; Frederick hit 12 – including a six to long leg – off his short-pitched second over and Hutton forthwith took him off. Before West Indies declared and won, Lock bowled Headley with his highly suspect faster ball and was duly punished for his temerity by the local umpire who 'called' him for throwing immediately afterwards.

In the second and third Tests, England played a more balanced attack; and strengthened the batting. Trueman, who did nothing in the two colony matches to justify his inclusion, and Moss who had done rather more, were left out. Bailey and Statham opened the bowling while Laker and, at Georgetown, Wardle as well, came in to support Lock with spin.

By the time of the second Test the atmosphere of the series had become unpleasant: stories were circulating about the bad behaviour of the English players who were undoubtedly angry at some umpiring decisions and some gratuitously offensive behaviour by local officials. With the benefit of hindsight it can be perceived that the roots of the bitterness and dissensions lay less in cricket than in the political and racial mood of the Caribbean.

There were, too, disagreements within the side: a tour can cruelly exacerbate minor differences. Some of the older players thought Hutton's approach too defensive; he thought some of of theirs careless. After the second Test defeat, a group of the senior members in a dinner-discussion decided to devote their attention to bringing the party more closely together – especially to removing the barriers between the older and younger generations – and to align the entire team solidly in support of the captain. Hutton, never a man voluntarily to share his troubles, listened to them with some relief, took their points and accepted their suggestion that he should adopt a more aggressive strategy. The general team-situation became healthier as a result; Trueman's position did not. Once he understandably provoked indignation by refusing – in loudly firm terms – to attend a cocktail party given for the team, because a local dignitary who would be present had described his bowling action as a throw. In a fraught and inflammable situation minor huffs were bound to be exaggerated. Three other members of the side recall disagreements – indignant replies to unfair allegations for which they were quite prepared to accept, responsibility and, if necessary, explain to authority – which were attributed to Trueman with no justification whatever. He would not deny, however, that the quick flare, the oath which let out bottled exasperation, made him more enemies of many potential enemies than a young cricketer could afford on his first tour. The wife of a high dignitary was not amused by some humorously flirtatious remarks.

At Barbados, his birthday was celebrated on the traditional – Saturday – 'club night' of MCC touring teams. The next morning an English 'county' lady told Len Hutton indignantly that she had been jostled in the lift by two of the MCC cricketers. Complaints like this horrified him : they were the very stuff of danger to his position. 'Who were they,' he asked :

'Trueman and Lock,' she said; whereupon the captain assured her the two would report to her in the hotel lounge at half-past-nine next morning to make their apologies. They duly appeared and the lady, whose services background had provided her with a searingly disciplinary manner, dressed them down for a quarter of an hour: they stood at silent attention until she had finished when they apologised with due humility and were dismissed. 'I thought you took that very well,' said Hutton. 'So do I,' Trueman replied, 'since it weren't us.'

Lock was three times 'called' for throwing in Barbados: he is an expressive man; he himself recalls his reaction: and this, too, was marked up against the 'troublesome pair'. In the match with British Guiana at Georgetown, when he was trying desperately to bowl himself into the Test team, Trueman was several times no-balled for dragging and had a number of lbw appeals turned down. One of the MCC players said to the umpire, 'What's wrong with these lbws? – they're dead right'.

'As a matter of fact,' the umpire answered, 'I can't see a stump.' He resented the laughter at his reply; and this incident, too, was held against Trueman. In this match an offensive remark was made to the umpire: Trueman, who was bowling at the time, insists that he did not make it, that he knows who did and does not propose to name him. Certainly the umpire went to Len Hutton and made a complaint which obviously disturbed him and caused him to change places with Suttle and field at mid-on, though he would never explain what happened. Realising that both his captain and manager thought he was responsible, Trueman insists that he went to the umpire and asked him if he had accused him, to receive the answer, 'I never said it was you. I didn't mention your name. I only said it was one of the four Yorkshiremen on the field.' The Trueman saga, as usual, has a version of it, which is that Fred turned to the umpire after an appeal had been refused and called him 'a cheating black bastard' and, when the official bridled, promptly said, 'And there's nowt o' colour prejudice in it – if you weren't black I'd have called you a cheating white bastard'. In the outcome the same two umpires were nominated for the Test: Hutton declared that neither was acceptable to him, his protest was upheld, and they did not stand.

By this time Trueman was extremely unhappy. He felt he ought not to have been dropped and he resented Statham being nursed – as he frankly was – and in effect being saved for Test matches. He did not know that it had been said of him early in the tour 'He won't be talking so much by the end of the tour – he won't have enough breath left'. He knew, though, that he bowled seventy more overs on the tour than any other pace bowler: even among the spin bowlers, only Lock – by eight – bowled more overs than he did in matches outside the Tests. He had never been in the tropics before; the sweat tumbled out of him; but he thundered on, and did not stop talking. He found no pleasure in the company of his team-mates apart from Lock and Evans. Despite their friendship his dislike of southerners dates from this tour. Above all, he believed that he was being blamed for offences committed by other people.

More than once he asked if he might have a word with 'the skipper' to resolve his anxieties and his puzzlement, only to be told 'Another time'. The other time never came.

The feeling within the rest of the party improved with the win at Georgetown, based on Hutton's splendid innings of 169, the work of all the bowlers, and outstanding fielding. Hutton, with admirable courage, insisted that his team remained on the field during a riot on the fourth day and the win set the series at two-one in favour of West Indies with two matches to play.

Trueman had recovered the fluency of his run up and, in the colony match against Trinidad, he took seven useful wickets and three catches. Less happily, he injured Wilfred Ferguson – the cheerful and popular leg-spinner. 'Fergie' was defending with Gerry Gomez to save the match when Trueman bowled him a bouncer: he ducked under it and, standing up, raised a general laugh by playing a mock hook at an imaginary ball.

F

Anyone could be forgiven for bowling a bouncer on the lifeless Port-of-Spain mat, but Ferguson was, after all, a number nine batsman. Trueman's next ball to him was both a bouncer and a no ball. Ferguson moved inside it to hook, missed, was hit in the face, and dropped. Fergie was an extremely likeable person: and the entire England side went to his assistance – except Trueman. There is, of course, an old story about the tough fast bowler who never sympathised with the batsmen he hit because that would only encourage them; and undoubtedly Trueman was acting out that character when he drew back, rolled his sleeves and scowled. Hutton was not playing and only after Charles Palmer went up and spoke to him, did he go and speak to Ferguson: but as soon as the batsman was on his feet again, he bowled him with a full toss of high velocity. The crowd hooted its displeasure and the island newspaper emphasised it next day. Embarrassed and emotionally tense, he violated Queens Park protocol at the close of play by running in ahead of the batsmen. The members in the pavilion received him in complete silence and pointedly applauded the remaining England players when they followed the batsmen. If this was Trueman at his least sympathetic, the rest of the party saw – as the public could not – his distress and his attempts, that evening, to get in touch with Ferguson who had been taken to hospital.

He was brought into the England team for the Port of Spain Test as part of a move to attack on that jute matting wicket where no Test had ever been finished since it was laid in 1934. An attack of Statham – who was injured – Trueman, Bailey, Laker, Lock, Compton – and, at the last, Graveney – could not prevent West Indies from making 681 for eight (Weekes 206, Worrell 167, Walcott 126) Trueman took one wicket – that of J. K. Holt – for 131 in thirty-three overs. After May, Compton and – almost – Graveney had scored centuries England still needed 21 to avoid the possibility of following on when Statham came in, last man, to Trueman. They put on 27 of which

Trueman made 19 and the result was the draw everyone had foreseen.

The fifth Test, played in Kingston, Jamaica, was effectively won by Trevor Bailey, who, after Stolleymer had won the toss and West Indies batted, took seven for 34, figures all but unheard of in a Test in West Indies on a wicket not affected by rain. Trueman, who bowled better than at any other time on the tour, supported him with two wickets in the first innings and, more importantly, those of Holt, Stollmeyer and Worrell in the second. Hutton made 205 and England won by nine wickets to come from two-none down and tie the series. Hutton who had overcome his early uncertainty, batted magnificently – 677 runs in Tests at an average of 96.71 – and accepted his position with such assurance that he was already shaping his team for Australia in the following winter.

Only Lock – by one – took more wickets in first-class matches on the tour than the twenty-seven of Trueman who batted usefully on the two occasions when he was needed to do so, and held some good catches. When the teams returned home he was the only member of the party whose good conduct bonus was withheld, and he was refused any explanation. This rankled with him for many years and, as late as 1964, in a BBC feature on his life, he pressed Len Hutton to give him the reasons. All he gleaned was 'These are in the official papers at Lord's: that's all I can tell you' – and that perhaps he appealed too loudly. He always felt that he was ill-used on the West Indian tour and that its consequences damaged his career. Certainly he never played in any of the eleven more Tests of the Hutton regime: and in only three of the next fifteen after May succeeded to the captaincy.

The apparently bright promise of the previous December had been swept away in bitterness. Trueman smouldered and over many following years some of his fury was worked off on batsmen.

CHAPTER EIGHT

Gathering Strength

It would have been difficult to convince Fred Trueman in 1954 that the best years of his career were still ahead, even though he worked hard in the attempt to prove it to himself. He smoothed out the last minor unevenness in his run-up and for the first time he took a hundred wickets in a season. He missed only one Championship match and played a valuable part in Yorkshire's revival – despite the frequent absence of Hutton through nervous strain or injuries – from the abject twelfth position of 1953 to that of runners-up to Surrey, who won for the third consecutive year.

This was the richest post-war period of English fast bowling. Trueman was competing for an England place with Statham, Tyson, Loader, Jackson and Ridgway in the faster category; while Bedser and Bailey, at lower pace but of high skill, were also available. Trueman knew well his main rivals and for several years he regarded every Yorkshire-Northants match as a personal contest between himself and Frank Tyson, whose description as the fastest bowler in the world he regarded as an affront. It was not simply a matter of impressing the selectors, but of self-esteem. On this issue Godfrey Evans, who kept wicket to both of them at all points of their careers, says positively that, on the issue of pace alone, Tyson, in the period from 1954 until he damaged his left heel in 1956, bowled faster than Trueman did at any time. He adds that, in other respects, Trueman might be Tyson's superior; speed is not the criterion – except to fast bowlers.

At Bradford at the end of June, George Tribe with his left-arm wrist spin bowled out Yorkshire: Tyson took none for 54. When Northants batted, Trueman had Dennis Brookes caught in the gully and then dropped one short to Eddie Davis who missed it, was hit on the head and retired hurt. Tyson – who made a capable 70 – and Jakeman, put on 100: but Trueman took four of the last five wickets – including Tyson's – for 11, just in time to give Yorkshire a first innings lead of five runs. Tyson countered by taking the first two Yorkshire wickets cheaply and finished with three for 36. Davis was caught at slip off Trueman before rain made a pitch for Close and Illingworth to bowl out Northants and win the match.

The next week Yorkshire went to Northampton where, as one of the players said, 'It wasn't so much a match between York-shire and Northants as between Trueman and Tyson: you could tell the crowd felt it and the players did, too.' Tyson put out Lowson at once; then Billy Sutcliffe played a sound and brave innings of 105. Tyson, coming back in the afternoon, bowled Illingworth, which let in Wardle who was, in the words of Jim Sims 'not frightened, but somewhat apprehensive'. When Tyson eventually managed to get at him he gave him the Trueman treatment, first a bouncer and then a straight half-volley which bowled him on the retreat. Trueman was the next batsman, and as he passed Wardle on the way to the wicket he remarked acidly, 'What a bloody stroke'. Within a minute he too was on his way back – bowled Tyson o – and when he reached the dressing room, Wardle was waiting with 'What a bloody stroke'. 'Ay,' he said, 'I slipped on that heap of shit you dropped in the crease'. This piece of repartee was admired in the dressing-rooms for months. Tyson had four for 63.

Night rain made a 'green' wicket next morning and Trueman slipped himself. As one of the Northants batsmen recalled, 'as if he was bowling fast leg-breaks: you couldn't lay a bat on him'. Dennis Brookes was caught at the wicket off a lifter for o: Peter Arnold, yorked – o – and Desmond Barrick bowled by a ball which pitched middle-and-leg and hit the off stump. Vince Broderick was caught at slip off Appleyard and Northants were eight runs for four wickets. They did not recover: the Yorkshire spinners wiped the slate.

In the four Tests against Pakistan, England used Statham, Loader and Tyson with Bedser and Bailey at fast-medium pace: Trueman, Moss, Jackson and Ridgway were never chosen. To give Loader and Tyson Test experience, Bailey and Bedser were rested at the Oval when Pakistan, in their first Test tour of England, won by 24 runs and drew the rubber.

The touring side for Australia had been taking shape in the minds of Hutton and the selectors since before the season even began; though it was disconcerting for Hutton to learn, after his efforts in the West Indies, that he had been harshly criticised for his captaincy there, and had been given the office of his greatest ambition – captain of England in Australia – by only one vote over David Sheppard. This was undoubtedly the main cause of his mental stress and illness. When the party was announced at the end of July the bowlers were Tyson, Statham, Loader, Bailey, Bedser, Appleyard, Wardle and McConnon. Fred Trueman heard the news in his home at Maltby and he and his family were not simply disappointed: they were shocked. His father was so angry that he suggested – and Fred did, in fact, say to a journalist who happily did not report it – that if he was ever asked to play for England again, he should refuse.

Next morning at Headingley he vented some of his indignation on the Derbyshire batting with their first three wickets in seven balls. The crowd were with him and, when Hutton misfielded, they barracked angrily. His outstanding performance – which remained the finest analysis of his career – came at the end of the season when Kent won the toss and batted on a slow damp wicket at the Crabble Ground, Dover. Trueman bowled the first ball of the match, Arthur Phebey edged it and Close caught it at slip. He maintained an immaculate length and

line – barely bowled a bouncer except at Peter Hearn – whom
he did not like (caught off the glove) – and in the last over of
the morning he bowled Ray Dovey. Kent were all out for
76 before lunch and Trueman had taken eight for 28. At Neath
he flogged life out of a wet, unsympathetic pitch and again
used admirable control to take seven Glamorgan wickets for
15 in the second innings of a game abandoned because of rain.

In innings after innings he took one, often two, important
wickets in his opening spell – thus the Champions, Surrey were
reduced to 13 for three and 5 for two at Bramall Lane – while
increased accuracy, enabled him to wipe out tail-enders with
swift economy. He and the medium paced Appleyard were an
immensely effective combination. They bundled out Hampshire
at Park Avenue for 72 and 89; Somerset at Taunton for 48;
Northants at Northampton for 90: Essex at Scarborough for
106; and a MCC team of England strength for 143 in the
Scarborough Festival. He was tenth in the national averages
with 134 wickets for 15.55 and his striking rate was a wicket
every six overs. With the batting ambition of every bowler, he
took great pleasure in scoring the first 50 of his county career,
against Gloucestershire.

In September he became engaged to Enid Chapman whom
he first met at a reception given by her father, then the Mayor
of Scarborough, at the Festival of 1950. When he was not
selected for the winter tour he received some financially attrac-
tive offers to make the trip as a press critic; but the Yorkshire
committee forbade it. He considered, but did not accept, the
suggestion that he should return to Lincoln City as a professional footballer. He filled in the winter he had expected to
spend in Australia by working as a furniture salesman and in
March 1955 he married and went to live in Scarborough.

In 1955 Fred Trueman played for England; he was picked
for only one Test of the rubber against South Africa, and then
as a replacement; but at least it brought him the relief of knowing that – although he had not been chosen against Pakistan in

1954 or for the tour of Australia – he was not permanently black-listed by the selectors.

There was much to do, for Yorkshire, who were again runners-up to Surrey. Hutton played in only ten matches, while Appleyard again fell ill and barely turned his arm after June. The main weight of the bowling fell on Wardle and Trueman with Close a rather expensive third string.

Wardle, in statistically his best season, took 195 wickets – more than any other bowler in the country except Lock (216). Apart from Sobers there can hardly have been a more giftedly versatile bowler than Wardle. Normally he was an orthodox left-arm finger-spinner of profound accuracy and subtle flight, able to contain the best batsmen on good wickets, an absolute destroyer when the ball turned. In this department alone he was so capable as frequently to displace Lock in the England team although he did not command the occasional high speed and exceptional spin which Lock then obtained by his admittedly unfair delivery. In fact, over the period when the two competed for an England place – from 1952 until Wardle's departure from the game in 1958 – they each won twenty-four caps.

Yorkshire traditionally prefer the precision of finger spin – especially on North country wickets which tend to be damp and slow – to wrist spin. Thus they did not employ Wardle as often as some counties might have done to bowl the 'Chinaman' – or left-arm bowler's off break – and googly. It is arguable that he was the finest bowler of this type cricket has known. His spin was acute; his googly well hidden; his flight varied; but most impressively he bowled it with greater accuracy than any other bowler of the kind has ever sustained. In South Africa in 1956-7 – when he performed the remarkable feat of taking 105 wickets on the tour – he virtually won the second Test Match by his own efforts when he took twelve for 89 with the 'Chinaman'. On other occasions, at Yorkshire's need, he used the new ball which he could swing to a good length at medium pace.

He was a brilliant field and a better batsman than his figures indicate. While he was capable of an orthodox innings, he could also hit spectacularly enough to rouse the younger element in the crowd to enthusiasm and sometimes devoted over much attention to that reaction. His clowning was often genuinely funny and superby timed; but sometimes he seemed too anxious for the crowd's approval. If it were suggested to him that he played for himself he would no doubt say that the same applied to the rest of the Yorkshire team of his day. He took 1,842 wickets in twelve years: and for more than a decade after he left Yorkshire he was still a superb and highly effective bowler – especially of wrist spin – for Cambridgeshire in the Minor Counties competition.

It was a serious weakness in Yorkshire's cricket that Trueman lacked a regular fast-bowling partner. When Mick Cowan – lively fast-medium left-arm – who was doing his National Service could get leave from the RAF, they were a highly effective and valuably contrasted pair. Their opening spell in semi-darkness on a lively pitch at Headingley that reduced Surrey to 27 for seven at the end of the second day was the decisive stroke that, to the anger of Stuart Surridge, enabled Yorkshire to beat Surrey and end their winning run of eighteen matches. Cowan, a jovial and amusing man, was promising enough to be chosen for the 'A' tour of Pakistan on the evidence of a few matches for Yorkshire spread over three years. Unhappily he injured his back on that trip, was flown home after four games and was never again fit enough to play a full season's cricket.

When Hutton returned from his great triumph of 1954-5 in Australia – winning the rubber by three Tests to one after losing the first – MCC took the unprecedented step of making him an honorary member while he was still an active professional player: and a few weeks later the selectors also made a unique move when they invited him to captain England for the entire coming series against South Africa. In fact Hutton never captained England again. He declared himself unfit for each of the 1955 Tests and Peter May took over the succession.

Tyson who had been such an outstanding success on the Australian tour and had destroyed the South African second innings with six for 28 in England's heavy win at Trent Bridge, was doubtful for Lord's Test because of a blistered heel and, in case he did not pass a fitness test, the selectors summoned Trueman to stand by. Tyson proved unfit; Trueman played and, when England batted, he kept an end closed while Wardle hit, in a last wicket stand of 22, a valuable proportion of a total of 133.

Statham bowled the first over for England, McGlew edged the first ball and Evans caught it. Of course Trueman, at the other end, had to prove everything in a moment. Over-eager and tense, he ran up to bowl his first ball, tripped and fell : next came a no-ball; then Goddard got an inside edge and Evans diving wide to his right, took the catch at full stretch. Before the over ended there was another no-ball and Cheetham was dropped by the wicket-keeper. At the end of the day Trueman had John Waite caught by Evans and that was the last wicket he took in the match. He was twice no-balled by Laurie Gray for dragging. This unsettled him, as it often did, and, attempting to alter the grounding of his back foot, he lost his line. On Saturday evening a near good-length ball from him stood up steeply and hit Jack Cheetham so violently on the elbow as to put him out of the remainder of that Test and the next two. In the second innings of South Africa Statham – bowling with utter accuracy and savage pace to the ridge end – had seven for 39; Trueman none for 39: Wardle took the other two wickets and England won by 71 runs. For the remaining three Tests the England seam bowling was done by Bedser, Tyson, Bailey, Statham and Loader.

When he returned to the Yorkshire side he reduced his run by six yards, in an attempt to correct his drag. There was no apparent loss of pace: indeed, he had a burst of twenty-five wickets in three matches. He finished the season strongly, too, and in August performed the hat-trick for the second time and once more he did it against Notts, with the wickets of three of their first five batsmen, Giles, Stocks and Cyril Poole. In the second innings he had Giles and Stocks lbw with consecutive balls and had a close appeal against Poole refused off the third.

He was ninth in the first class averages with 153 wickets at 16.03, though only 120 of them were in Championship or Test cricket. Again his striking rate was under seven.

In January 1956, Len Hutton announced his retirement. He had consulted a specialist about the back trouble that had plagued him for three years and had been told it was not likely to improve. He was not prepared to be less than he had been and he left the game. Norman Yardley, too, retired and Billy Sutcliffe took over the captaincy of Yorkshire. Although he was not an outstanding player, his batting improved appreciably with experience and he was a keen, cheerful, considerate captain. He was constantly and unfairly compared with his distinguished father, Herbert Sutcliffe: none made the comparison more often or more cruelly than the Yorkshire crowds. Several of the players disapproved of his appointment and gave him little help: in consequence he resigned after two years. In this, his first season, unreliable batting, poor fielding and lack of spirit brought Yorkshire down to seventh place in the Championship.

It was a poor summer for Trueman. He suffered considerable pain from a strained left side which frequently rendered him completely unable to bowl and once reduced him abjectly to vomiting. Worried consultants at one point of the season recommended that he should not bowl at full bore for at least six weeks. At other times he was troubled by sciatica and blistered feet. Moreover he was in trouble for dragging in the first match of the season and reverted to the old long run. Constant wet weather made it a spinners' year. The fact remains, however, that in thirty-one matches he took no more than fifty-nine

wickets; his striking rate rose above nine; in nineteen Championship fixtures for Yorkshire his figures were thirty-three wickets
at 25.48 and he was eighth in the county averages. Although
he played in two Tests against Australia he was brought in only
when Tyson or Statham was unfit.

He could not feel that he shared in the triumph as he could
in 1953. In the first innings of the Lord's Test – Miller's Match
– he had twenty-seven overs and took two for 54. In the second,
although a burst blister had deeply wounded his left heel, he
bowled with immense fire and precision, and in one of his
characteristic spells – four for 38 – brought Australia to 79 for
five and wiped out their advantage. Benaud regained it the
next day with a bold innings of 97. Trueman eventually had
him caught at the wicket but by then the initiative had passed.
Miller and Archer broke down the English second innings and
Australia won their single Test of the summer – on the only
good wicket of the series. In his first innings – of seven – Trueman drove Archer, who was of quite lively pace, along the
ground through the covers for a four of quite memorable power
and majesty.

At Leeds he was quite unenthusiastic about the action of the
Chairman of selectors, G. O. Allen, in taking him to the nets
in front of a fairly large crowd, putting a handkerchief down
around a good length and directing him to see if he could hit
it; and recommending him to bowl a fuller length to the Australians. Lock and Laker won that game for England. Trueman
took one for 19 and one for 21: his best moment of the match
was when, in Laker's leg trap, he anticipated Miller's stroke,
moved to his left for the catch, the off-break turned more than
he expected. The snick went fine and, twisting back off balance,
he made the catch by trapping the ball between the middle
finger and wrist of his right hand. Miller still remembers it with
rueful surprise. At Old Trafford, Statham came back; at the
Oval, Tyson. In any event Laker, with forty-six wickets in the
rubber, and Lock with fifteen, needed little assistance from the

faster bowlers though Trueman with nine at 20.44, was second
in England's Test averages.

Yorkshire were conscious of their need for pace bowling support for him. When Cowan broke down with a recurrence of
the injury he had suffered in Pakistan, they tried Bob Platt,
who worked intelligently to vary his formerly rather monotonous
inswing with a leg-cutter; the unusually tall Philip Hodgson who
never quite realised his early promise; Peter Broughton, quite
fast if not always accurate with a rather unprepossessing action;
and the strong and splendidly equipped Mel Ryan. None quite
satisfied them. Platt was the most successful; but the slower
men, Illingworth, making his first substantial impression with
his off-breaks, Wardle and Appleyard, did most of the summer's work.

In Yorkshire's match with the Australians at Sheffield Trueman bowled Rutherford with the first ball of the match: Burke
was lbw to the second ball of his next over; and when Appleyard
had Harvey lbw the touring side were three for 3. He knew few
such moments that year. Nevertheless, on one of the rare occasions when he had the assistance of Cowan, he rose to the
challenge of contention with Tyson.

There had been no real confrontation between them in 1955
– the first Northants match was played on a slow turner and
neither he nor Tyson took part in the second. The two counties
met only once in 1956 – on a typical Northampton wicket,
where bowlers had to make their own pace. Northants batted
and Trueman bowling, he believes, as fast as ever in his life,
had his usual fortune of this summer. He beat the bat and
stumps as well; was snicked a couple of dozen times – three
times to hand, only for the catches to be dropped – and to his
frustration and fury took only the single, late wicket of Keith
Andrew for 63 runs.

From this innings comes one of the anthology pieces of True-
maniana when, after a batsman who had already twice, unconsciously, deflected him between pad and leg stump, made

an on-side push and scored four to third man off the outside. Fred finished his follow-through, stood hands on hips and said in a tone of loathing and contempt, 'You've got more bloody edges than a broken pisspot'.

Tyson, flogging life out of the reluctant pitch, had five – including that of Trueman, bowled 11 – for 60; and Northants took a first innings lead of 9. In his always encouraging double harness with Cowan, Trueman set about the Northants second innings. Arnold was yorked – o – Cowan, having caught Dennis Brookes at short leg for three, chipped in with Jock Livingston taken at the wicket and, when Lowson caught Reynolds off Trueman at slip, Northants were 23 for four. A few minutes afterwards a lifter from Trueman hit Desmond Barrick on the hand and he did not bat again in the match. Trueman's final analysis of five for 34 was his best of the season and he savoured it deeply.

He had not done enough – and he knew it – to be chosen for the 1956-7 tour of South Africa; the seam bowlers picked were Tyson, Statham, Loader and the invaluable Bailey.

His suspicions were to some extent allayed when Walter Robins and the secretary of MCC, Ronnie Aird, stated specifically that the selection of the team had been based on current assessment of merit; that no restrictions had been placed on the selectors: and that there was no question of discrimination against Trueman. So he set off less unhappily than he might have done on the short tour of India for the Bengal Cricket Association's two Silver Jubilee matches, in which he took eight wickets and was top scorer in one innings with a violently struck 46 not out.

Those who looked only at figures wondered whether, aged twenty-six at the beginning of the 1957 season, he had declined from his earlier ability. He and Yorkshire believed not: that his quality was beyond question. Their only doubts concerned his fitness – the distressing side strain which had now worried him for three years.

He returned to the new regulations designed to prevent time-wasting and, since he had been criticised for the length and leisureliness of his walk back, decided to use an exact eighteen-yard approach, forsaking his former scuffling allowance.

It was a reassuring season for him from the start. After an early spasm of stitch, all the symptoms of side-strain disappeared. He took twenty-seven wickets in his first four matches; and played in all five Tests against West Indies; Tyson, who had a hundred-wickets season for the first time, did not appear in one. Trueman was fourteenth in the first-class averages (two of those above him took less than twenty wickets) with 135; and top of the Yorkshire bowling, though he produced most of his best performances outside the county. Almost a quarter of the overs he bowled were maidens; his striking rate was only fractionally above one in six; and he knew where he was bowling.

It was a season of unrest for his county: although they finished third in the county table, they were 122 points behind the Champions – Surrey again. During the summer some of the county players circulated a petition asking for Billy Sutcliffe to be removed from the captaincy. Trueman refused to sign it; in August Sutcliffe announced his resignation; and Willie Watson, the strong pillar of the batting since Hutton's retirement, also left to join Leicestershire who could satisfy his justified aspirations.

At the start of the Test series with West Indies, on a true Edgbaston pitch Ramadhin threw the England batting into almost superstitious doubt and with seven for 49, wrecked their first innings. They were all out for 186 and West Indies made 474. Trueman yorked Pairaudeau early in the innings and next morning, while Walcott was off injured, he bowled Weekes; but it was heavy going on a slow wicket. Both Walcott, who made 90, and Worrell (161) suffered muscle strains and Pairaudeau acted as runner for Walcott for three-and-a-quarter hours and Worrell for five, so that for most of Friday and Saturday there seemed always to be two batsmen – one tall and one short – at

one end of the pitch. As the umpires, Emrys Davies and Charles
Elliot, in their white coats, walked out through the players'
dining room at the end of the Saturday tea interval, they were
followed by a small, white-coated pavilion attendant, whereupon
Trueman remarked 'I see you've got your runner with you,
Charlie': timing and picture were both perfect. Ramadhin
brought England in their second innings to 65 for two, only for
May and Cowdrey in one of the major technical feats of modern
Test cricket, to master him on Monday and Tuesday, by treat-
ing him simply as an off-spinner. He bowled a record number
of ninety-eight overs in that innings. They put on 411 for the
fourth wicket – also a record – and destroyed the little man's
power for ever.

The recovery to a total of 583 broke the cool, West Indian
certainty and Trueman, intuitively aware of this advantage,
drove fiercely into their second innings. He had Kanhai caught
at slip and bowled Pairaudeau for only 9 runs before he handed
over to the spinners, Lock and Laker. They brought the innings
down to 72 for seven: there was no time – nor, in a way, need
– for more: by the end of this drawn match England had taken
an initiative they never lost for the rest of the series. They won
by an innings at Lord's, where Trueman had four for 103 and
hit three sixes in an over from Ramadhin.

The Trent Bridge Test saw one of the finest sustained bowling
performances of Trueman's life and the first major success of his
partnership with Statham. The wicket was the classic stage
which Trent Bridge prepares for batsmen, and England handi-
capped themselves from the start by leaving out Lock from their
summoned twelve and using an attack of four bowlers, three of
pace, and only one spinner of Test quality – Statham, Trueman,
Bailey and Laker – with Don Smith of Sussex as an extra seam
bowler. In the event, Bailey tore muscles in his back so that,
in heat wave conditions, the others had to shoulder some heavy
labour, and even Graveney was called in to help out.

May had won the toss and England – largely through

Richardson (126), Graveney (258) and May (104) – were able
to declare at 619 for six; West Indies were 295 for three on
Saturday night. There was some rain on Sunday but Worrell
remained as permanent evidence that the – covered – pitch had
not been affected. He became the first West Indian batsman to
carry his bat through a Test innings (for 191 not out). Once
more Trueman got his blow in first. He dropped the third ball
of the morning short; Weekes played a hook, was past the ball
before it arrived and it ran off his glove into the stumps. That
struck the spark. Trueman tore in; the ball never jumped, and
he used the bouncer only often enough to induce uncertainty.
Despite Worrell's unworried example, the West Indian batsmen
were simply demoralised. His opening spell – an immense
physical effort – was ten overs: six maidens: 20 runs: five
wickets. The quality of his attack was thrown into sharper
relief when Ramadhin found conditions comfortable enough to
stay three-quarters of an hour with Worrell while the fast
bowlers rested. Statham ended the innings at 372 and May
enforced the follow-on.

Two wickets to Trueman – Sobers and Kanhai: two to
Statham – Worrell and Weekes – and one, Walcott, to Laker,
and West Indies, 89 for five, were apparently losing at mid-
afternoon on Monday, when that merry and highly talented
cricketer, Collie Smith, settled in to play one of the most important innings of his sadly short life. England dropped catches:
one off Statham, two – including one by Trueman – off Laker;
Smith made 168, and with Atkinson and Goddard (both dug
out by Statham) played West Indies into and down Tuesday
against the three England bowlers and their irregular assistants
on a still good pitch and in extreme heat. In that last afternoon
May went to Trueman soon after taking him off and asked him
for another flat-out spell while there was still time to win. As
his bedraggled and sweating fast bowler wearily put out his
hand for the ball he said cheerfully, 'Come on, Fred – England
expects, you know'. 'Oh, does she, skipper, is that why they

G

call her the mother country?' Eventually he bowled Collie Smith (with a slow off-break) and Ramadhin: Statham ended the innings, but by then England needed 121 runs to win in an hour and, against Worrell and Gilchrist, they never approached such a rate.

The analysis of Trueman and Statham in this match – against the background of pitch, weather and lack of assistance – are measure of their strength, skill and application.

	First innings				Second innings			
	O.	M.	R.	W.	O.	M.	R.	W.
Trueman	30	8	63	5	35	5	80	4
Statham	28.4	9	78	1	41.2	12	118	5

Their figures became even more impressive by comparison with those of the opening pair for West Indies – who used altogether nine bowlers –

	First innings				Second innings			
	O.	M.	R.	W.	O.	M.	R.	W.
Worrell	21	4	79	1	7	1	27	0
Gilchrist	29	3	118	0	7	0	21	1

England won each of the remaining three Tests by an innings: Trueman had four good wickets at Leeds, where Loader did the hat-trick; and though he picked up only one on the spinners' killing ground at the Oval, he took more in the series – twenty-two – than any other bowler.

At the Oval, earlier in the year, he had underlined his vastly improved control and technique in Yorkshire's match against Surrey. For some incomprehensible reason – presumably myopic remote control by a committee in Yorkshire – Cowan, who was in the party, was left out of the side. Surrey won the toss and batted and, in a temperature of over 90 and high humidity, Sutcliffe led out a team in which Trueman was the only bowler of more than medium pace. On a comfortable batting wicket

Surrey made 365: Trueman, shirt and flannels clinging to him, bowled twenty-two honestly fast overs and took five wickets – including four of the first six batsmen – for 67 runs.

One of the most revealing incidents of his career comes from the Scarborough Festival of this season. Godfrey Evans captained the Players against the Gentlemen, lost the toss and, on the first morning, when the Gentlemen batted, went out uneasily aware of the problems posed by the fact that a south-westerly gale was blasting across the ground with such force that it threatened to blow in the front of the pavilion and that his opening bowlers were Tyson and Trueman.

'Fred,' he said, 'I want you to open,' threw him the ball and then, as Trueman walked away towards the Trafalgar Square end, 'No, not that end, the pavilion end'.

'If you think I'm going to bowl into a wind like this bugger after the season's work I've done you can bloody think again because I shan't': and he stood, hands on hips, at his most evidently truculent.

'But I want Frank to bowl with the wind because he's faster and he might knock one or two down quickly.'

'He's only bloody faster than me if he's bowling with this sodding gale and I'm going against it.'

'He won't bowl now,' said Johnny Wardle with a chuckle.

'If you don't bowl, Fred,' said Godfrey quietly, 'we shall all have to go off.'

Fred scowled 'Don't be bloody daft; gimme t'ball'.

'Good – and I won't keep you at it – just a couple or three overs'll do, but you'll bowl well into it.'

Trueman bowled with no little skill, using the wind to hold up his out-swinger; and he had a catch dropped. Meanwhile Tyson, extremely fast with the wind at his back, clean bowled Billy Sutcliffe for one. As they passed after Fred's third over Godfrey said 'Thanks Fred – get your sweater! have a rest and I'll give you a go with the wind presently.'

'Nay, that's all right, I'll carry on – we're doing well.' He put in another three steady overs; Tyson bowled Mike Smith – also for one – at the other end and the opening had been successful.

Perhaps he thought Godfrey Evans would not stand up to him; however that may be, they became firm friends, roomed and dined together on tours. That did not prevent Trueman from cracking three of Evans's ribs with a beamer and apologising with, 'Sorry about your ribs Godders – really I meant to skull you – anyway, why didn't you put your bloody bat there?'

In 1952 Len Hutton had said that Trueman needed another four or five years to mature. The judgement was accurate: he reached the high plateau of his skill late in the summer of 1957. He needed one ingredient to bring him to his best; and he had never really known it in his entire cricket career. He had known captains who could be firm, wise, helpful or kind; and captains who knew cricket: he had never known one whom he felt knew him – Fred Trueman – until he played under Ronnie Burnet.

Burnet, formerly captain of Yorkshire second XI, succeeded Billy Sutcliffe in 1958. He was a less accomplished cricketer than Sutcliffe: much less so than Norman Yardley. On the other hand he was tenacious, determined and perceptive. He had never played a first-class match in his life until, at the age of thirty-nine, he captained Yorkshire against MCC at Lord's and went out to bat with Yorkshire 83 for five. He took no part in the last day of that game because of an attack of gastro-enteritis: and was injured in the next – with Cambridge University – so that he did not appear in a Championship match until the season was five weeks advanced.

Many who thought that Yorkshire ought to have abandoned their old shibboleth of an amateur captain and appointed a professional did not appreciate that Burnet's appointment was not a technical one. The Yorkshire committee had recognised that the trouble in their cricket was not solely a matter of batting, bowling or fielding.

Burnet was appointed to put heart and discipline into the

Yorkshire team and he did so firmly and at calculated cost of some fine talent. In the August of 1958 John Wardle, already selected for the MCC tour of Australia in the coming winter, was informed that his services were required only until the end of the season. He was given the decision by the Yorkshire secretary, John Nash; but when he asked permission to stand down from the August Roses match because he had undertaken to write newspaper articles critical of other Yorkshire players, it was Ronnie Burnet who told him to go, and never to return to the Yorkshire dressing-room. The Yorkshire committee ended his contract; and MCC cancelled his invitation for the Australian tour. So, by the end of the 1958 season, only Trueman, Close and Vic Wilson remained of the team of 1950.

Bryan Stott, Ken Taylor and Doug Padgett as batsmen; Jimmy Binks the wicket-keeper; Ray Illingworth, all-rounder; and Burnet had been capped. Phil Sharpe had shown early promise as a batsman with a century in his third match; David Pickles looked a likely fast bowler, and Don Wilson was in mind as Wardle's successor. No one, however, could have rescued Yorkshire's season from the weather. On twenty-four days they had no play at all; in six matches not even a first innings decision was reached; two were abandoned without a ball being bowled: the conditions for the Notts fixture at Hull were so bad that the third day was given up on the second.

When play was possible, Trueman bowled sharply and well. He was fourth in the national averages with 106 wickets at 13.33; first in Yorkshire's Championship figures with 62 at 11.91 – better than one every six overs. Ronnie Burnet gave him the assurance he needed – needed not to be a good bowler, but to be secure; he encouraged him, praised him; told him what to do and, in return, Trueman gave the best he had to offer – cricket and loyalty.

After his hat-trick in the MCC match at Lord's, rain prevented any play in the county's first Championship match – against Hampshire at Bradford – until the third day. Ingleby-

Mackenzie's declaration left Yorkshire 55 minutes to make 106: and, after a brisk beginning by Stott and Taylor, Trueman's 58 not out in half an hour – with three sixes and six fours – won the match with five minutes and seven wickets left.

Derek Shackleton was generally regarded as one of the most difficult bowlers to hit but Trueman hammered him with unique regularity, relying on Shack's constant length and his own propensity for pull-driving on the rise. Shackleton's seven overs in this match cost 64 runs.

Trueman had six for 35 in the two innings against Somerset: nine for 58 in the defeat of Surrey and even the lack of regular new ball support – no other seam bowler took more than twenty-two Championship wickets – could not impair his zest.

In so wet a summer, most of the bowling in the Test series with New Zealand was done by the spinners; but he played in all five Tests and had five for 31 in the first, at Edgbaston. At Lord's he made a remarkable catch when, anticipating D'Arcy's defensive back stroke to Laker, he stepped up from square short leg and, as the ball dropped from the bat, caught it with his hand against the batsman's foot. D'Arcy stood for seconds in complete disbelief before he walked away. At the Oval he pull-drove that talented and philosophical leg-spinner Alec Moir cross-batted for three long sixes in the course of his 39 not out made in twenty minutes.

He no longer felt a boy or a stranger in the Yorkshire or England dressing room. He was fit; the distressing bouts of stitch had ended: he had settled to a steady weight of about fourteen stone, and he felt his own man. He had been chosen for the tour of Australia – as he knew he would be – and he was happy. He was, in fact, about to enter on that period of mature achievement when he was, to use the Yorkshire expression, 'in his pomp'.

CHAPTER NINE

In His Pomp

For six splendid years Fred Trueman strode the cricket world with a not unjustified swagger. People's eyes turned to him in a cricket match; he sensed it, and gloried in it. He slouched back to his run-mark and, when he paused dramatically before moving in, he had his audience in his hand as surely as the ball; and he knew it. When he squatted on his haunches, relaxed but poised, at short leg, his cap deliberately crumpled on his head, a blade of grass between his lips, nattering at the batsman, he was relishing being what he was and where he was — an England cricketer in a Test match, or a Yorkshireman playing for his county.

When he came to his peak, during Ronnie Burnet's period of captaincy, he was an utterly committed Yorkshire player. Previously there had been doubts; he had been ill at ease with team mates, uncertain of himself and of them. By 1959 only Close, with whom he was on gruffly straightforward terms, and Vic Wilson, whom he then found easy — and an asset as a catcher at short leg — were his equals in seniority. The remainder of the team were his juniors, to whom he was affable. Sometimes those who felt the strain of matches and wanted to be quiet might disengage themselves from conversation; but the old hostility had gone and he was now as much at his ease as his nature was ever likely to allow.

Apart from his natural aptitude, he became a great fast bowler for two reasons. The first was his single-minded determination to be exactly that; the second, his immensely strong body. It was not merely powerful, it was quite phenomenally solid, without observable weakness; and it proved magnificently durable. Like S. F. Barnes, Derek Shackleton and Brian Statham, he bowled himself fit. Dexter's 1962-3 team to Australia travelled from Aden to Fremantle on the *Canberra* where one of their fellow passengers was Gordon Pirie who offered to organise physical training for the team. He suggested that Trueman, as a bowler, needed exercises to strengthen his legs. 'My legs?' said Fred, 'they've carried me through over a thousand bloody overs this season – and they've never let England down yet – which is more than can be said about some.' Then, with a cold look overboard, 'Canst tha' swim?' The conversation ended. His legs were like tree trunks; and he bowled himself fit – that is to say fit for bowling, which is a peculiar and unique kind of fitness. There is no known training for a man who, wearing heavy – in this case steel toe-capped – boots, thick socks, long flannel trousers and a shirt thick enough to guard against chill, to walk a hundred and fifty yards, run a hundred and fifty yards, with six violent peaks of muscular action, in five minutes; rest for five minutes and do it again, and at the same intervals for an hour; then become semi-active and, at any moment, when the muscles have set or while they are still tired, be suddenly called upon to go through the entire routine again. All this may be demanded in the cold of an English spring or the high heat and humidity of Brisbane: and the same amount of applied strength, the same precision, is expected of him in either circumstance. It is an illogical form of activity which may account for the fact that there is no logical form of preparation for it. On the other hand, during his later years, if Trueman had three days off, he needed half an hour's bowling before he was loose.

His approach, though long and menacing, was controlled, its length and rhythm changed at different periods of his career as he sensed the changing nature of his demands from it. Its co-hesive quality was to be seen, even at his fastest, in the monu-mental steadiness of his head and shoulders which remained

as firm during his run-up as if he were standing still. If these
rocked it meant that he was weary, about to lose rhythm, length
and line; but, despite the weight of the demands put upon him,
that rarely happened.

He, Statham and Tyson were a remarkable set of contempo-
raries: the finest fast bowlers of more than a quarter-century,
they were born within eight months – and less than sixty miles
– of one another: Tyson at Bolton on 6 June 1930, Statham at
Gorton, Manchester, eleven days later; Trueman at Stainton
in the West Riding of Yorkshire on 6 February 1931. The only
comparable incidence of time place and quality in cricket history is the birth of Frank Worrell, Everton Weekes and Clyde
Walcott within an even smaller area of Barbados in the seventeen months between August 1924 and January 1926.

Statham – 'the Whippet' – the most finely drawn of the three
was also the most accurate – probably more consistently so than
any other bowler of his pace in cricket history. Tyson, who
entered first-class cricket later and left it earlier than the other
two, was, for his brief peak period, beyond all question the
fastest bowler in the world. He planned his career, acquired a
university degree and went consciously into being a fast bowler,
content that he could spend himself in one splendid bonfire of
effort and, when the flame died, turn to the security of teaching.
Fred Trueman came into county cricket before either of the
others and left it after them; he had a career of twenty years
as a fast bowler and he expressed himself – or his different selves
– in every moment of it. He was the most resourceful, violent
and unpredictable of the three: Statham was accurate; Tyson
was fast: Fred was everything.

Oddly enough, though Statham formed with Trueman England's longest-lasting fast-bowling pairing; and shared Tyson's
great series in Australia in 1954-5 and his destruction of South
Africa at Trent Bridge in 1955; the three played only once in
the same Test, at Adelaide in 1959, when Tyson had declined
from his high peak and, though the other two had better figures,

Australia still made 476 and 36 for no wicket and won by ten wickets. Trueman and Tyson played together in only four Tests – all in Australia and New Zealand in 1958-9 – and in all but one Trueman had the better figures.

Trueman needed a strong body for, lacking Statham's capacity for relaxation or Tyson's cool objectivity, he suffered from the stresses of cricket. Fortunately he was a long sleeper.

Fred Trueman was not a level bowler. He could always be a good one; at times he was lit by the fire of greatness: and the most stirring memories of him recall days when, in face of completely discouraging opposition, conditions and state of the game, over-bowled and ill-supported, he tried harder than any captain could fairly ask, and sometimes succeeded beyond the bounds of reasonable possibility. On the other hand, there were occasions – rare, but undeniable – when he turned it in. A dead pitch could depress him, as it did in the Old Trafford Test against Australia in 1961 when he had figures of one for 55 in fourteen overs and none for 92 in thirty-two overs. Taking his sweater from the umpire he said to Peter May, 'Let Closey bowl'. May, never strong about Trueman, did put Close on. More often Trueman was moved to the heights: though no one could tell what might provide the impetus.

He could be encouraged – Burnet could do that better than anyone else – a brilliant catch off his bowling would fire him – or he could be angered: being hooked or edged, or simply played with apparent ease might do it. Once, in 1960, he bowled all morning on a plumb Portsmouth wicket which had no real help for anyone but such favour as it had was available for spinners. A little after the middle of the second morning Yorkshire had scored 399 for seven – Bolus 146 not out, Close 102 – with minimum trouble and declared. In the afternoon Marshall and Gray made 118 for the first Hampshire wicket with similar ease before they were out to the spin of Wilson and Close: Horton and Baldry went steadily to tea. During the tea interval Fred was in some discomfort with an attack of the squitters.

Some of the Hampshire players were unwise enough to laugh at him. He went out in awful anger, which was unusual, for, despite impressions to the contrary, he was not an angry man – most of his fierce expressions and gestures were more dramatic than profound – took the new ball, rolled his sleeve and bowled out Hampshire twice. In ten overs he took six wickets for 11 runs and hacked them down from 166 for two to 191 all out. They followed on that evening and with a night's rest in the middle he tore apart their second innings with six for 28 in 19.3 overs. His match-figures were twelve for 62 : consider those of the other seam bowlers in the match – Cowan one for 70; Heath three for 125; Shackleton two for 98; Baldry none for 5.

No one, however, knows what kindled the fires when, at Edgbaston in 1963, on a pitch which had proved useless to Hall and Griffith, he rose up in splendour and bowled out West Indies with a final explosive five for none in nineteen balls, and brought England their only win of the series.

The kindling could be sudden and unexpected. All that any-one knew was that suddenly he was going eagerly back to his mark; there was a belligerent spring in his run, he came over like a storm-wave breaking on a beach, and followed through with so mighty a heave that the knuckles of his right hand swept the ground. Where previously the ball had curved off the pitch calf-high, it now spat to the hips or ribs: wicket-keeper and slips moved deeper; the batsman, who had seemed estab-lished, was late on his stroke; and the whole match was trans-formed.

This was the essence of fast bowling. Yet it is a mistake to think of Fred Trueman as simply a bowler of speed. It is known that he commanded out-swing, in-swing, that he had greater control with the yorker than any other bowler of comparable pace in modern times except, perhaps, Lindwall; that he had the knack of hammering the ball into the ground – as Keith Miller and Ray Lindwall in 1953 encouraged him to do – so that he gained not only lift, but also movement off the seam.

Indeed, he shared with Lindwall the rare ability to 'do' as much as a fast-medium bowler at fast bowler's speed. On 'green' wickets he shrewdly kept the seam straight and let it do its own unpredictable work. So ball after ball would, by his natural tendency, whip away from the bat and then, suddenly, beyond his control – 'I don't know, so how can the batsman?' – one would cut savagely back into the stumps. Although he could not command that ball it was always possible because of his method.

He was proud when he first took wickets with his slower ball. Batsmen, though, remembered his faster ball: he would seem to be bowling at full speed when suddenly one would come through an unaccountable and undetectable foot quicker, and defeat the stroke. He had, too, something of a dossier-system of the batsmen of his experience. He knew their weaknesses and their strengths; those who would push forward and those who would go back to his first ball at them; those who felt outside the off stump; those vulnerable on the leg; the shrinkers and the hookers; all were filed in his memory. He was more subtle than those who did not know him ever realised. He was, in the words of S. J. Perelman about an altogether different person, 'crazy like a fox'. In yet another strength, he believed implicitly that he was too good for any batsman; and sometimes he convinced the best of them that he was right.

Only a few great batsmen could play Trueman when he was 'in his pomp' with consistent confidence and certainty: he would admit May, Cowdrey, Sobers, Walcott – on West Indian wickets – Weekes, Sobers, the two Simpsons – Bobby and Reg – Insole, Washbrook, and one man who never appeared in a Test, the resolute Brian Reynolds of Northants. Only the two Simpsons were opening batsmen of Trueman's maturity (Washbrook had by then dropped down the order) for when he was fresh and the ball was new, he probed technique, temperament, courage and speed of reaction with so sharp a point that few regularly passed the examination.

A tendency to bowl too many bouncers remained his weakness. Although he could push a man on to the back foot in anticipation of it and then fool him with a yorker, he did not do it frequently enough. The bouncer was his exclamation mark, and he exclaimed to the end of his career, even when its bounce was as predictable as its incidence.

The temptation to use him was irresistible; he was shock bowler and stock bowler in one; capable of containing a strong batting side in conditions to its liking, always with the possibility that he might bowl them out at the same time.

Even in this period he was not a regular choice for England. He was dropped from the team for the last Australian Test of 1961 – when he admitted the selectors' justification – and did not make the tours of Australia 1954-5, South Africa 1956-7 and 1964-5, India-Pakistan in 1961-2 or India in 1963-4. From the beginning to the end of his career as an international cricketer England played 118 Tests and he appeared in only sixty-seven of them. Thus his record number of Test wickets – 307, an average of over four-and-a-half a match spread over thirteen years – becomes even more remarkable.

It is striking, too, that Statham played his first Test in the series before Trueman and his last in the one after Trueman finished: and that he played in 70 out of 123 – a slightly smaller proportion than Trueman's. Again the coincidence of their careers is striking: no other English fast bowler endured as these two did: while from other countries, only Lindwall – who also had thirteen years of Test cricket – compared with them.

By 1959, Tyson's ankle injury had slowed him and Fred Trueman was without doubt the fastest bowler in England. So far as the world was concerned the Australians Rorke and Meckiff – whose actions were, at mildest, doubtful – Davidson; Wesley Hall of West Indies and, now that Heine had gone, Neil Adcock from South Africa, disputed the title. In England his closest challengers were Brian Statham, Peter Loader – of the dubious bouncer – Harold Rhodes and David White: only Brian Statham for completeness of technique and David White, on his day for sheer pace, cast the slightest doubt on his national title.

So he assumed the mantle of authority with a rare blend of violence, humour, tolerance, experience and brilliance; authority, however, never included conformity; he was not the establishment's man; he could still four-letter-word himself into trouble, still slash the establishment with the sharpest edge of his tongue. Sometimes, too, in his impatience, he had to resort to the beamer, dispatched straight at the point between the batsman's eyes; and once when he was offered even greater violence in return, he not only desisted but doled out a couple of drivable half-volleys by way of compensation. Such generosity was un-usual. He normally had bouncers, yorkers and boxers ready for those – generally southerners and fancy caps – who were on his grudge list; and Yorkshire can attribute their run of four Championships in the five years of Fred's 'pomp' largely to the fact that, at the pinch, he could usually summon the knowledge, resource and application – and, above all, the pace – to remove any batsman.

It is true of all bowlers, but more so in the case of Fred Trueman than most, that when he was taking wickets he was never tired; once he mounted the kill he could not be pulled off. When, in 1960, he was – for the only time in his career – the first bowler in England to a hundred wickets, he came to York-shire's match with Warwickshire at Bradford nine short and closely pressed by Jackson for the distinction. On the first morn-ing he went, as usual, into the visiting dressing room and chatted up his opponents with his latest stories, opinions and humour, which they accepted with the enjoyment of most teams who did not live with him six days a week. At about eleven o'clock he eased himself off the table to go and change with the words 'Oh, yes, and I only want nine wickets to be first to a

hundred – so you buggers can start drawing short straws to see
which one I don't bloody well have'.

The Warwickshire batsmen were duly impressed; but Yorkshire won the toss and, after a first day shortened by rain,
batted until the middle of Monday before they declared at
304 for nine. Trueman emphasised the validity of his boast by
having both Billy Ibadulla and Arnold Townsend taken in the
gully from lifters in his first over. The spinners, Jack Birkenshaw and Don Wilson, worked their way through the middle
of the innings and he had a couple of catches dropped before
he took his next wicket – Jack Bannister, edging to the wicket-
keeper – and, when Warwickshire followed on, he still wanted
six more wickets and he was tiring. Nevertheless, once Cowan
had put out their fellow Yorkshireman, Norman Horner, Trueman swept away Arnold Townsend, Mike Smith, Billy Ibadulla
and Ray Hitchcock and Yorkshire claimed the extra half hour.
Trueman now was clearly spent and Vic Wilson told him to
take his sweater. He protested, was allowed another over, which
proved little more than fast-medium – and had another catch
dropped – before he came off in high dudgeon and Birkenshaw
took his place. 'I'll never bowl for Yorkshire again – and don't
send me back to leg slip because if you do I shall drop anything that comes near me – like these bastards have been doing
off me all day'. Five minutes later he picked up a glorious swoop-
ing catch off Barry Fletcher from Jack Birkenshaw's bowling
– at leg slip.

As he threw it up he said 'I'll have another over for that'
and promptly bowled John Kennedy. So three wickets were
left for the next day and he wanted two of them. When play
started late, after rain, Bannister and Geoffrey Hill proceeded
with steady competence to bat until lunch and double the score.
They even batted on into afternoon before Cowan bowled Hill
and Fred, who had refused to be relieved, launched himself
at John Fox. He was flagging now and it was a wide, and not
very fast ball – the last of an over – that Fox chased and edged

to Jimmy Binks to let in Ossie Wheatley, one of the world's natural number elevens. Bannister took a single off Illingworth and so – less wittingly – did Wheatley, before Trueman began his twelfth consecutive over of the day. He was weary but Wilson would not have dared to take him off: he was not to be baulked of this easy victim – though it was by no means certain that he could muster the fast, straight ball that was invariably enough for Ossie Wheatley. He gathered himself, rushed in and bowled: the ball pitched short and at no great speed, wide of the off stump; Wheatley went to 'shoulder arms' and let it pass, but he did not do so quickly enough: the ball hit his bat on the backlift and flew between slips and gully for four. While the field shook with laughter Trueman stood, hands on hips, scowling at the batsman. 'Well,' he said, 'that's the first time I've been left alone for four.' Wheatley was not the most gifted or intrepid of batsmen and, while he observed Trueman's exhaustion, he was not certain that he would not now be given a bouncer of greater pace than his batting ability warranted. So, as Trueman moved up Wheatley began to inch away. The ball proved to be a straight full toss but, in the moment before it would have hit the bails, Wheatley's bat, coming from the opposite direction, demolished the wicket completely and, by a fraction of a second, the dismissal became 'Wheatley hit wicket bowled Trueman 5' instead of 'Wheatley bowled Trueman 5' (his batting average for the season was 4.94). F.S.T. was first to the hundred wickets and the afternoon dissolved in talk and celebration.

England's first choice fast bowler; the main strength of the Yorkshire attack; trusted and encouraged by his captain; at ease with his fellow players; feeling the power of his bowling and the strength of his position – he became easier than he had ever been since the Yorkshire club left him forgotten in Maltby with his torn thigh ten years before.

He walked into the dressing rooms of Yorkshire's opponents with little of the old doubt, less thought that he was a hated

'Yorkie'. They were – until they had the bat and he had the ball – fellow cricketers – and an audience: his jokes were fresh to them; he was entertainment; a 'Fred session' became a recognised feature of fixtures with Yorkshire. This was the full flood of confidence and contentment and it was confirmed or perhaps simply reflected – by achievement.

He could not now escape the fact of being a public figure even if he had in the past tried to ignore that aspect of his life. His image now took on some consistency of shape through his personal reaction to public pressures. He regarded himself as an eleven-thirty to six-thirty worker with such variations as playing hours might demand. In that time he was happy to bowl, bat and field to the utmost of his ability; entertain unconsciously – sometimes – by his emotional reactions to play and events; and, more often, deliberately, in clowning, responding to crowd-clamour and generally dramatising himself. When play ended he believed that his duty to the public ended also: that his life was his own and that he was entitled to privacy – even in public places – and he never really recovered from his annoyance at the discovery that this was not so.

He was not only a public figure, he was the most effective gate-attraction in English, and probably in world, cricket. Understandably he was in immense demand, particularly for Sunday matches for charities – usually other cricketers' benefit funds – and so long as those cricketers were not on his hate-list, he would go to trouble to help. With some trepidation I asked him to help with a Sunday match for Peter Sainsbury's benefit. It was to be played fifty miles from Yorkshire's fixture at Bournemouth and an invitation to lunch before, and the local buffet afterwards seemed little inducement to offer. He agreed to come cheerfully and at once. When we mustered for lunch an early arrival from Bournemouth remarked 'Fred might be a bit late; when I came in at half-past-three this morning he was just going out for the second time.' It was a chilling moment: the poster and press announcements that Fred

H

would play would, we knew, have put several hundreds on the gate – and to fail to produce the prize attraction would be to invite trouble for future matches. Ten minutes later – exactly on time – Fred arrived, swept and garnished. He was polite and amusing to the ladies; funny and kind to the children. At the match he bowled fast and – to a youngster – slow; he played some brilliant fielding tricks, hit four huge sixes before he gave away his wicket; sold raffle tickets determinedly; suffered some bores gladly; had a few glasses of beer afterwards and, waving away thanks, left for Bournemouth. As he went one player's wife turned to her husband with 'And after all you've said about Fred Trueman! – no one could possibly have been more helpful or more polite – you men are worse than women'.

County cricketers – by no means all off the top playing level – remember Fred for kindnesses of this sort. In his early days he could be bloody-minded; in his pomp he could afford to be generous and he often was – to his friends.

There is a widely accepted picture of Fred with a heavyweight pipe of tobacco and a pint of beer. He does smoke a pipe, but not heavily – or his wind would not have held out as it did; and he does not drink heavily. It is true that he can be seen for long periods with a glass; that he sometimes lays on a 'cod' drunk act; and at times after a few drinks he has been more belligerent than most. For my part I have known some cricketers who did get drunk – some of them frequently; but I would not put Fred Trueman in that category; he belonged rather in the steady beer-drinker class. He suffered more than most of his kind from drunks and clever chaps who decided that they could use his Christian name and would shout across a bar 'Hello there Fred, boozing again, eh?' – and they thought him rude when he resented it – as he infallibly did. He thought he should be able to sit and drink in a bar or dine in a restaurant, alone or in company, without being interrupted every two or three minutes by a stranger who, cutting into thought, conversation or eating, asks for an autograph 'for my boy Willie' – no one ever met anyone who wanted an autograph for himself. This is a difficult aspect of public life and I have observed it striking the same cord of irritation in two cricketers as different as Sir Donald Bradman and Fred Trueman; I have seen them both put up a defence of their privacy which was not only misunderstood but resented – and reported with embellishments within moments.

He resented, too, the pack of small boy autograph-hunters who pester sportsmen – sometimes almost beyond bearing – for signatures on grimy scraps of paper which clearly are not really wanted; or over and over again for 'swaps'. His annoyance in this instance was frequently that of a physically tired man who had given the day his energies and now wanted rest and to follow his own bent: he did not hesitate to tell them to bugger off or take other spectacular if improbable methods of leaving.

In company Fred Trueman could become excited, lose his judgement of what to say, when and how loud to say it; and most of his gaffes were committed out of embarrassment. As an after-dinner speaker he could be entertaining and usually was; he could misjudge his audience and make both them and himself subsequently miserable.

He did not follow the leisure-pattern usual among cricketers who tend – at the away matches that are half their summer life and from time to time in the winter – to flock together. From the early days of antipathies he tended to go out alone. He was often invited out to the homes of non-cricketers: more often he ended up in a bar or a restaurant where his gregarious nature usually immersed him in conversation.

This was his real relaxation and recharging. He could not face the early bed of some fitness enthusiasts. His body was strong and needed no excessive rest; but his mind buzzed with anxieties, uncertainties, angers, hopes, problems, ideas which would be stilled only by the sleep of the truly tired. He tired his mind by parties, talk, company – of a widely assorted and often unexpected kind – and when he went to his room he was ready to sleep. He lay late abed in the morning, partly because he was that kind of sleeper but also from the sense of the luxury, which comes to all those brought up in working class homes, of not having to be early up and off to work.

The rather shaggy outfits of his youth gave way to restrained suitings, fastidiously neat, trousers sharply creased; shirts gleaming, shoes highly polished. This was his chief extravagance; and he is not an extravagant man: though he has a leaning towards sporty motor cars. Like most who have known the pinch or have grown up in its reflection, he meant to be safe. 'I'm going to have a hundred thousand,' he said one day and, as someone smiled, 'and I'm halfway.'

He did better than most out of cricket; justly enough since he played it better than most; he did well out of the side-products of being a famous cricketer, which are often larger than the direct earnings; and he was there at a time when the rewards for cricketers could be high. Fred enjoyed his 'pomp' – and made it pay.

CHAPTER TEN

The Unexpected

Ever since he was left out of Hutton's 1954-5 party, an Australian tour had been something of a symbol in Fred Trueman's mind and he regarded his selection to go under Peter May in 1958-9 as both an achievement and a compensation. He accepted that his progress at cricket had to be made the hard way. He did not expect to be offered anything for the sake of his bright eyes: he expected no more from 'them' than he had earned beyond question.

The 1958-9 tour was disappointing in many ways. Advance assessment of touring teams is invariably wrong; and so it proved in this case. May's side was said to be as strong as any sent by England in modern times. In the event it lost the rubber and The Ashes – which England had held since 1953 – by four Tests to none. The defeat was the more bitter for those who were not satisfied with the methods of some of the Australian bowlers. Meckiff, first in the Test bowling averages, was subsequently 'called' for throwing; Rorke, who bowled from a great height and undoubtedly unsettled the main English batsmen, had a jerky action and such a huge drag that he often delivered from eighteen yards. As a result of Watson's knee injury and Subba Row's broken wrist, two of the left-hand batsmen deliberately selected to deal with Alan Davidson's fast left-arm bowling appeared in only two Tests between them.

The tour manager was F. R. Brown, of whom Trueman had no previous acquaintance. It was unfortunate that the manager began it, before the team even set out, with 'Any trouble from you and you're on a slow boat home'. Trueman had played in five of the first six matches of the tour before an attack of lumbago kept him out of the Queensland fixture and the first Test and he was told 'You'll have to get yourself fit or you must go home; we don't want unfit people on this trip'.

This was, at best, extremely bad applied psychology. No one who knew Trueman could imagine him being anything but eager to get into a Test Match if he could; and the final figures show that he bowled more overs on the tour than anyone except Lock.

He was so enraged that he declared he would go home instead of continuing on the New Zealand part of the tour; fortunately for his future, and the team, Peter May persuaded him to change his mind. His suspicions and his hackles bristled. People met him, with none of the other cricketers, in snooker halls – he is an extremely capable player – or he went out visiting unaccompanied. Nothing, though, ever diverted him from his purpose of bowling fast. He knew, too, that he had some friends of influence in Godfrey Evans and Trevor Bailey, who argued his rights.

So far as the Australian crowds were concerned, he was the most popular member of the team. He had none of the characteristics that Australians most dislike in the English; and his clowning was invariably good-humoured, if not always subtle. At Hobart he and Tyson were barracked for bowling bouncers to a batsman who would not 'walk' but elsewhere he was always sure of a cheer when he came out to bat.

The pitches had little of the life Tyson and Statham had found and exploited in 1954-5. Trueman, for his part, had to learn to bowl habitually shorter than the full length he generally used in England where the ball moves more in the air and, by 'digging in', extort such movement and pace as he could from the pitch.

Although Australia won the first – Brisbane – Test by eight wickets, that could be attributed to the collapse of England's batting. Statham and Loader had done enough to keep their places for Melbourne with Bailey as third seam bowler and, though Trueman had five for 46 and four for 33 – numbers three, four, five in three overs after tea – in the South Australian match, he and Tyson were left out. Another Australian eight-wickets win at Melbourne, although Statham took seven for 57 in their first innings – brought Trueman in for Loader at Sydney.

He had McDonald dropped by Swetman in his first over and it is impossible to estimate the psychological effect of the miss: an early wicket often gave him a considerable fillip; a dropped catch could depress him. He bowled only twenty-two overs on the match and took Mackay's wicket for 46 runs. An inadequately covered pitch helped spin : Benaud took nine wickets, Laker seven and Lock four, in a fairly even draw.

Trueman did nothing finer on this trip than in the second Victoria match when, in a temperature of 109 degrees in the shade on the Saturday and Monday – some kind of high temperature record for Melbourne – he bowled thirteen eight-ball overs and, in a total of 286, took five for 42. It was such a performance as wins a Test place.

At Adelaide the Ashes were at issue. With Laker unfit to bowl, England switched to a full pace attack with Statham, Trueman, Tyson and Bailey, plus Lock.

May won the toss and put Australia in: the early life soon dried out of the wicket and they batted until the third morning for 476. Trueman had a fine spell of three wickets – including Colin McDonald, the top scorer – for 22 and, once more in great heat, bowled altogether 30 eight-ball overs for 90 runs and four wickets. The English batting was again disturbed by Rorke and destroyed by Benaud: it was simply not strong enough – Trueman suffered a 'pair' – Australia won by ten wickets and took The Ashes.

At Melbourne, after three consecutive Test ducks, Trueman scored 21 and 36, including a spectacular off-drive off Rorke;

and he took four wickets for 92; but Australia won once more; this time by nine wickets.

In New Zealand, where England at last won a Test – and drew the other – there was some statistical comfort for a few of the bowlers who had remained – especially Lock – and, with an lbw decision against Eric Petrie, the wicket-keeper, Trueman took his hundredth wicket in Test cricket.

At the beginning of the 1959 cricket season Yorkshire seemed about as likely to win the County Championship as England had looked to lose The Ashes eight months before. In the county side of 1957 Watson, Lowson and Sutcliffe scored 3,052 runs between them; Wardle, Appleyard and Cowan took 225 wickets; and at that time it could be reasonably expected that all six would be playing for the county in 1959. In the event not one of them appeared in any county match that year. Meanwhile the highly promising David Pickles had lost his bowling action and took only thirteen – expensive – wickets. Of the ten capped players, six had reached that seniority only since the start of the 1957 season.

The batting flourished, if in a way not always associated with Yorkshire cricket. Bryan Stott, Ken Taylor, Doug Padgett, Ray Illingworth, Brian Close and the uncapped Brian Bolus all played valuable forcing innings. As one of the closest observers of the county's cricket remarked 'third afternoons were usually more convincing than first mornings'. Seven players scored nineteen centuries, which is not a large number by the standards of some of the powerful Yorkshire batting sides of history who could not have done what this side did to win the title in its last match, at Hove. They needed 215 in 105 minutes to beat Sussex – a rate of about 8 runs an over. 15 runs – 13 of them to Stott, the left-hander – came in the first over: 50 in twenty minutes. In the main stand of the innings Stott (96) and Padgett (79) made 141 in little more than an hour, Trueman hit 11 in the final flurry, and the 'impossible' objective was reached with seven minutes to spare.

The players themselves realised – though they did not relish being reminded of the fact – that they might not be as gifted as some of their predecessors: nevertheless they had won – handsomely. Surrey, Champions in the seven preceding seasons, Northants – once with and once without Tyson – and Gloucestershire each beat them twice. They lost both the matches of their 'Western tour' to Gloucestershire – who created a new record by dismissing them for 35 the lowest total in Yorkshire's Championship history until Hampshire reduced it to 23 in 1965 – and Somerset. Decisively, though, they won six of their last nine matches – the last one with such panache as deserved a Championship.

The bowling was splendidly sustained. Trueman was top of the averages and took most wickets; he had ninety-two at 18.60: in Championship matches his striking rate was one in 6.3 overs: a quarter of his overs were maidens. Of the county's seven defeats, five occurred during his absence at Test Matches; of their fourteen wins he played a decisive part in seven, made an important contribution to two others, and almost won a tenth.

Others balanced the team's bowling economy. Illingworth, making a steady advance in his transition from batsman-occasional-seam-bowler to off-spinner-all-rounder, performed the double. His advance to maturity; Bob Platt's combination of bite and steadiness; and the hard work of Close were the main factors in the rehabilitation of the bowling after the loss of two England spinners. Don Wilson, asked to fill the important boots of Wardle, took fifty-three Championship wickets and against Notts performed the first hat-trick of his career and the only one of the season.

To complete the picture, Jimmy Binks was already as good a wicket-keeper as could be wished, and the catching was splendid – seven men apart from Binks took twenty catches in the season for the county. Burnet's captaincy probably was conclusive. The players under him were young and might easily have been discouraged or thrown off nervous balance. All but Trueman, Vic Wilson and Close had played under him regularly in the second XI and he watched their development with something more than interest while they, for their part, found him sympathetic and gave him their enthusiastic support. It was important that, while he was himself a modest performer – and did not pretend otherwise – he made it clear that what he had to offer did not compete with the skills of his men. He was there to observe, encourage, to take technical advice while making the ultimate decision himself. He had in effect carried out an effective exchange of spirit for talent: the long period of 'failure' – which, in Yorkshire means not winning the Championship – had ended.

After five consecutive away matches, the team returned to Yorkshire as Champions, were cheered out at Scarborough, where they met a strong MCC side and beat them in a fashion characteristic of the best of their season. Set 260 to win in two-and-a-half hours, Stott, Padgett, Close and Illingworth made the runs with twenty-five minutes and seven wickets to spare.

The Champion County v. the Rest match at the Oval threatened anti-climax when the Rest made 384 and Yorkshire followed on 224 behind. Again the batting rallied; in the second innings Vic Wilson scored 106; Stott, Close, Bolus, Illingworth and Trueman (45) chipped in and raised a total of 425. Then, appropriately on that famous spinners' killing ground, Close and Illingworth, supported by spectacular catching, took nine wickets between them with their off breaks and won the match by 66 runs.

Fred Trueman made a fine and penetrative start to the season and, if he tired towards its end, that was understandable in a man who after a hard winter in Australia came back to bowl 1072 overs – more than anyone else in the country of remotely comparable pace – in the domestic season. Certainly he never lost heart nor fire. He felt himself deeply committed to

Yorkshire's attempt upon the Championship, on grounds of personal loyalty to Ronnie Burnet, his unity with his new and younger team mates, his general Yorkshire feeling – which might be simply called 'Yorkshireness' – and all the subjective loyalties of his youth and family. There was, too, the sensation of having reached the actuality of a youthful dream which had been partly obscured by years of disillusionment. This was one of the most warming experiences of his life. He was intrigued by one of the many congratulatory telegrams that awaited the team when they reached Scarborough – it read 'Best wishes and well done, from Johnny'. No one ever knew whether or not it came from Johnny Wardle.

In November, the celebration over, Ronnie Burnet resigned from the captaincy; his job was done. For a man of forty-one the strain of playing first-class cricket after entering upon it late in life was considerable: and he stated his simple wish to make way for a younger man.

His successor was Vic Wilson, a good choice; a loyal careful professional; the first professional captain Yorkshire had appointed since before Lord Hawke needed to be cautiously chosen. A huge, rosy-faced, strong man from Malton in the North Riding; he came from farming stock and looked it. He was a useful, sometimes spectacular, forcing, left-handed batsman when the ball did not turn (off-spinners could torment him when it did) and his huge hands and fearless approach made him a fine short-leg fieldsman. The team were happy at the appointment.

For Trueman the Test series – against India – was largely of arithmetical interest. He could hardly expect to repeat the spectacular success of the 1952 series and, on far better pitches, he did not. He was content to take more wickets – twenty-four – than anyone else on either side, and at the cheap rate of 16.70. His constant victim of 1952, Pankaj Roy, did a little better this time: but it was an Indian side of small aspirations; and, as might have been forecast, became a record breaking touring team by losing all five matches of a Test rubber in England. It was little short of ludicrous that eight England batsmen should have averages of 50 or over, first among them Brian Statham who was only out once in Tests.

This series established the Trueman-Statham partnership. Hitherto they had generally been alternatives to one another, alongside Bedser or Tyson. Now those two and Loader were out of the selectors' minds and Bailey was regarded as a third seam bowler – as distinct from an alternative opener in an attack emphasising spin – the Yorkshire-Lancashire pair began their long run in double harness. They had shared the bowling three times in West Indies in 1957-8; twice against New Zealand in 1958; and twice against Australia in 1958-9. Now, if injury had not kept Statham out of the third and fourth Tests, they would have had their first full series in partnership. They were the two chief wicket-takers – Trueman twenty-four and Statham seventeen – and Trueman bowled more overs – 177 – than any other English player. He began the series by breaking down the first Indian innings at Trent Bridge; and he and Statham finished off that match when, with the new ball, they took the last five Indian wickets for 26 runs in little more than an hour. At the end, Trueman had four for 24 and three for 30 at The Oval. Both he and Statham realised that they would face sterner opposition in the West Indies during the winter tour ahead. Only one visiting team – Ian Johnson's Australians of 1954-5 – had ever won a Test rubber in the West Indies. Two England sides – Freddie Calthorpe's in 1929 and Len Hutton's of 1953-4 – had drawn their series: the other two had lost.

Few people were prepared to give this 'new' England team any chance of winning. A whole generation of great players – Lock (temporarily while he made an honest man of his action), Graveney (also eventually to return), Laker, Bailey, Evans, Loader, Wardle, Watson,. Richardson and Tyson – had gone. It appeared when the team sailed that almost everything depended on the four experienced players, May and Cowdrey among the batsmen, Trueman and Statham of the bowlers. None of the other batsmen had ever made runs against major Test opposition and the spin bowlers Allen (who had yet to play a Test) and Illingworth were unproved deputies for Laker, Lock and Wardle. The batting emerged as massive and by no means dependent on May – who was never really fit – and Cowdrey.

Dexter, Mike Smith, Barrington, and Subba Row all made Test centuries; and at the end, Jim Parks, who was coaching in Trinidad was brought in as wicket-keeper, scored 183 in his 'practice' innings against Berbice, and a most important 43 and 101 not out in the fifth Test.

It was the happiest and most successful of Fred Trueman's tours; it was the first in which he revealed his full ability away from English conditions; and he was happy in a side captained by Peter May – and, after he became ill, by Colin Cowdrey – and most important, managed by Walter Robins. The two were obviously going to react strongly to one another's strong character: their natures made it impossible that they would be indifferent: fortunately they liked one another. Robins, a perky, quick-witted person with a sense of mischief and of humour, admired Trueman's skill and his determination, and valued his stamina. He talked as much as Trueman – gave him crack for crack – and treated him with precisely the blend of encouragement and leg-pulling that made him content; not simply content but eager to reflect his pleasure in cricketing effort.

England had the satisfaction of winning the series and of establishing the core of a capable team. They could only regret the riot that interrupted the second Test, in Trinidad; the 'bumper war', which Hall and Watson conducted more intensively than Statham and – surprisingly – Trueman (several English batsmen wore improvised body pads as protection against the short-pitched ball on the line of the body); and the prevalence of illegal bowling actions not only of first-class players, but in club play and even among children.

Six important years older than on his previous visit, with a substantial record of achievement behind him; a senior instead of a junior player, Trueman had the confidence to 'attack' the crowds psychologically. He responded to them, defied them or clowned. Quite early in the tour he could 'handle' a hostile spectator-reaction merely by cupping his ear with his hand as if he could not hear it. At bottom those volatile crowds recognised and hailed another extrovert; and, particularly away from the pressures of Test Matches, he delighted them with by-play – and ultimately with penetrative fast bowling.

He made a stimulating start with five wickets (three in one over) for 22 in the second innings of the first match – against the Windward Islands at Grenada – only to labour on the Bridgetown wicket – none for 110 in twenty-four overs in the first innings; none for 16 in three in the second – when Nurse made 213, Sobers 154, Barbados declared at 533 for five and won by ten wickets. Coming off in the rain at the end of that match, Statham fell and damaged a hamstring and was unable to play in the Test that began four days later.

Again the pitch was lifeless: England scored 482, with centuries by Barrington and Dexter: then Sobers (226) and Worrell (197 not out) slowly set a new record for a stand by two West Indian batsmen against England – 399 for the fourth wicket – and the game was drawn. In all, 1,116 runs were scored and eighteen wickets fell. At the end of the fifth day – the third of the West Indian innings – Trueman had bowled thirty-seven steady, accurate overs in unhelpful conditions, taken one wicket (Kanhai, bowled off his pads) for 69 – bowling against sadly defensive batting; and dropped two catches. On the next day, maintaining spirit and stamina he improved to four for 93 as the game dragged on to the predictable draw.

He had two wickets in the first colony match with Trinidad; did not play in the second, and Statham was fit to open the bowling with him in the second Test, also at Port of Spain. May won the toss; England batted and were 57 for three before Barrington (121), Smith (108) and Dexter (77) in their con-

trasting styles – especially against the bouncer – hauled them up
to 382. Despite some retaliatory bumpers from Trueman, the
West Indian opening pair, Hunte and Solomon, batted out the
second day 22 for no wicket. The third day – a Saturday – was
decisive in the match and the rubber; and distastefully important in West Indian cricket history.

There was a hint of sap in the wicket and of humidity in the
air and Trueman and Statham bowled in the finest joint operation they had yet carried out. Statham employed the flawless
hammering accuracy of his greatness: Trueman, more ambitious,
at full pace, pitched up out-swingers, occasionally made one
move back; threw in a yorker or a slower ball. May set four
short legs and four slips for him. He caught Hunte at short-
leg from bat and pad off Statham; then had Kanhai lbw with
a yorker and Sobers caught at slip, where May pushed up a
fierce slash for Barrington to wait until it came down. David
Allen threw out Solomon and, immediately before lunch,
Worrell, trying to drive a full length out-swinger from Trueman, edged it: Roy Swetman, the wicket-keeper, scooped it up,
wide down the off-side. West Indies were 45 for five: Trueman
had three for 12 in eight overs: the unfortunate Statham no
more than one for 20.

By afternoon the ground was uncomfortably overfull, partly
with people who had scaled the walls; there was tension in the
air and the players were conscious of it : in sharp contrast to the
two previous days, hardly a bouncer was bowled. The cricket
itself was quiet after lunch; in the entire middle period, only
one wicket fell – Butcher lbw to Statham.

After tea Trueman, bowling like an old soldier into the wind,
moved one back to beat Alexander: 94 for seven. Almost at
once Charan Singh, the Trinidadian slow-left arm bowler was,
as he subsequently confirmed, unquestionably run out. A
steadily intensifying shower of bottles – many of them already
broken – was thrown on to the ground, and a section of the
crowd swarmed on, intent on reaching the umpires. Gerry Alex-

ander, the West Indian captain, Learie Constantine and Sir Edward Beetham, Governor of Trinidad and Tobago, attempted to smooth over the matter. It ran too deep for that: there had been much drinking and gambling; Charan Singh was a local boy; he had been given out by an umpire – umpires command little popular affection in the Caribbean – and West Indies were losing. Deeper than all this was the climate of social dissatisfaction. Trinidad was deeply aware of the finer gradations of colour; the difference with England was even more profound.

The English team – Trueman and Statham, armed with a stump apiece guarding its flanks – made an orderly way to the pavilion. Police escorted the umpires. There was no more play that day. On Monday Trueman (five for 35) and Statham (three for 42) finished the job they had begun. May did not enforce the follow-on. After Illingworth (41) and Trueman (37 including 18 from an over by Charan Singh) had put on 60 in half an hour the English declaration set West Indies 501 to win in ten hours. Kanhai's century did not prevent Statham, Allen, Barrington and Dexter from bowling them out and giving England the game by 256 runs.

The third Test at Kingston, Jamaica, was taut and constantly shifting, never foreseeably the drawn match it proved. Cowdrey scored a century in a shaky England first innings: West Indies – Sobers lbw Trueman 147 – lost their last seven men for 24 and still led by 76 on the first innings. Another responsible piece of batting by Cowdrey – 97 – was followed by near collapse: West Indies needed 230 in 245 minutes to win and set out to make them. Statham was hobbled by blisters on his feet and was brave to bowl at all. Grafting through a sweltering afternoon, Trueman hit McMorris's off stump at 11; Hunte and Kanhai struck at a run a minute. Trueman bowled Hunte; Sobers was run out; West Indies needed their last 130 runs in as many minutes. Trueman, again with the body-action break-back, bowled Nurse; then yorked Kanhai: West Indies – 175 for six –

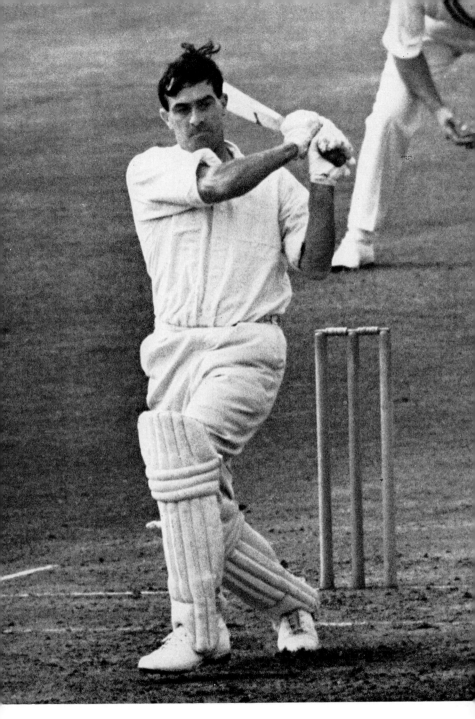

Wearing a track through mid-wicket

Maximum Effort, v. West Indies, Edgbaston, 1963

fell 55 runs short. Trueman's four for 54 had effectively saved the match for England.

He laboured with intelligent accuracy in the heavy scoring draw at Georgetown, with three for 116 in forty overs in the only West Indian innings. Hereabouts Peter May fell ill; Cowdrey took over the captaincy; Brian Statham flew home because his son was ill and Fred Trueman, to a delight he could not conceal, was appointed senior professional. It is convincingly related that when he was informed of this elevation, his first comment was, 'Then t' first thing these buggers'll have to do is cut out t'bloody swearing'.

He was a tired man in a tired team by the time they came to the last Test – the second at Port-of-Spain. He kept runs down with shrewdly controlled tactics but, apart from bowling Worrell at an important stage of the first West Indies innings, he had little edge and, without the help of Statham, he was grateful to help England hold on for the fourth draw of the series which gave them the rubber.

When he left home for the West Indies in December he weighed 14 stone 8 pounds: he returned 13 stone 3 pounds. In the Tests he bowled most overs and took more wickets – twenty-one – (Statham was next with ten in his three tests) than any English bowler had ever done before in a rubber in the West Indies. On the entire tour he bowled more overs than anyone except Illingworth and, by fourteen, took most wickets. He looked and admitted he was – knackered.

CHAPTER ELEVEN

A Thousand a Year

It was long said that, 'The more bowling you give Fred True-man, the better he bowls', or 'Fred has to bowl a lot to bowl at all'. Three of the captains who, technically, knew him best – Len Hutton, Vic Wilson and Brian Close – disagreed with that theory. Each of them preferred to keep him sharp, bringing him on for short spells and soon resting him: thus, they argued, he was always available, at his fastest, to enlarge any break-through.

The fact is that he constantly bowled more overs than any other true fast bowler. In each of the four English seasons from 1959 to 1963 he bowled more than 1,000 overs; in five others, more than 800; with a major tour before the sequence began, another at the end and two – one serious and one social in between. The work sheet of his entire career shows 15,976 six-ball and 494 eight-ball overs, for 2,304 wickets; for one who never deliberately reduced his pace below fast, this was a tower-ing, controlled, physical performance.

The most productive of the four four-figure seasons was 1960 when he was the first man in the country to a hundred wickets – reached in that hilarious moment in the Warwickshire match at Bradford – and finished fourth in the first-class bowling averages with the highest tally of wickets – 175 – both of that season and of his career: they cost only 13.98 each. Often using a shortened run, though with no observable diminution of pace – he simply seemed more concentrated in application of power – he was Yorkshire's keenest weapon in retaining the title –

with 132 at 12.79 in Championship matches – and England's most successful bowler against South Africa.

He and Statham virtually won that Test rubber: it was the first time they had ever bowled together in every Test of a series. England took the rubber outright by winning the first three Tests, in which the two fast bowlers took thirty-nine wickets between them; and they shared fifty-two (Statham twenty-seven, Trueman twenty-five) at an average of less than 20 each in the five games.

At Edgbaston, England – with five current county captains in the team – took first innings for 292; and when South Africa batted, on the second afternoon, Cowdrey threw in Statham and Trueman in a vast sustained effort. Statham bowled from half past three, with only the tea interval for rest, until twenty-five past six. Trueman – who took his 150th Test wicket when Parks caught McGlew – had a two-hour stint. South Africa, 114 for five on the second evening, were all out for 186 on Saturday – four wickets to Trueman, two to Statham who ended the innings by throwing out Tayfield from third man. The second England innings, with Pullar injured, never took firm root against the contrasted bowling of Adcock – tall, fast, and in Trueman's class as a bowler of bouncers – and the mercilessly accurate flighted off-spin of Tayfield. Only the tail end batting of Peter Walker (37, in his first Test), Trueman (16 from an over of Tayfield) and Statham lifted England from 118 for seven to a final 203.

South Africa needed only 310 to win. This time Statham made the early inroads and they were 5 for two; Pithey, Waite but essentially the stroke-maker, Roy McLean, brought them to 120 for three by the fourth evening and with seven wickets left they needed 190 on the last day. Trueman bowled the first over of the morning to the batsman of South Africa's hope, McLean: he held back his second ball, McLean hit across it and was lbw – that ball decided the issue.

The remaining batsmen were never allowed to engineer a

recovery. Trueman, Statham, Illingworth and Bob Barber – in a subtle and steady spell of leg-spin – accounted for all but John Waite, and England won by 100 runs.

The Lord's Test probably had more dramatic event – by no means all of it concerned in the course of the match – than any other ever played. In the attempt to rule out the possibility of play being affected by the notorious, alleged 'ridge' at the pavilion end the pitch was moved a yard nearer than usual – or traditional – to the pavilion. England batted comfortably enough to 347 for five when Mike Smith who, after a competent innings, wanted only one for his century was caught by the wicket-keeper, John Waite, off Geoff Griffin.

Griffin, a pleasant, modest, fair-haired, young fast-medium bowler from Natal, had already been 'called' for unfair delivery a number of times by six English umpires, one of whom – Frank Lee – was standing in this Test. In this match he had been the first man 'called' for throwing in a Test in England. It had happened eleven times – and he had had Cowdrey caught at slip – before he took Smith's wicket with the last ball of an over. In the next over – bowled by Goddard – Peter Walker hit two long, on-side sixes and, with a single, faced the beginning of Griffin's over: He played back to the first ball which nipped and flicked off the bails. Griffin was 'on' a hat-trick. The batsman was F. S. Trueman. McGlew summoned up a close-catching field: Trueman scowled intimidatingly at them, took a terrific swing and lost his middle stump. Griffin had taken a hat-trick: the first by any South African in Test cricket or by anyone in a Lord's Test: it was his last Test and the last first-class match in which he bowled in England.

Cowdrey declared next morning at 362 for eight and the Lord's Test Saturday crowd watched the unfailingly exciting spectacle of a batting side routed by fast bowling. The bowler was Statham. He bowled twenty of the forty-four overs in the innings and took six wickets – five of them in the first seven places of the order – for 43 runs. He struck at the South African

batting with the relentless persistence of a pecking gull. His stock
ball moved in to the bat off the pitch; but from time to time –
often enough to breed doubt in the batsmen's minds – one
angled away. Moss – the third pace bowler always indicated for
a Lord's Test – earned his four for 35: Trueman – none for 49
– had an unusually bad day. South Africa followed on and,
before a storm ended play at five o'clock, Statham bowled
McGlew in the second innings.

On Monday he maintained the same precise, pitilessly applied
pressure. This time Trueman joined him and they battered the
innings down to 63 for five. Colin Wesley and John Fellows-
Smith made a late gesture but there was no real likelihood that
South Africa could escape defeat, and they did not. Statham's
match figures of eleven for 97 were the best of his Test career
and by any English fast bowler of the post-war period until
then.

When the Test ended, a little before half past two on Monday, an exhibition, over-limited match was played. In the course
of it Syd Buller called Griffin for throwing four times in his
first over: and he finished it bowling underarm. It was all as
sad as salutary. Trueman gave it a final gloss with one of the
biggest sixes seen at Lord's within living memory – on to the
roof of the pavilion.

The South Africans went to the third Test still depressed by
the Griffin affair, and even more by the conclusions they drew
from it. A fair – and, by recent standards, fast – Trent Bridge
wicket afforded enough bounce to encourage bowlers and stroke-
making batsmen. England, winning the toss again, batted and,
mainly through Cowdrey and Barrington, attained the semi-
respectability of 287, a little before lunch on Friday.

Then Cowdrey – another captain of Hutton's persuasion –
once more threw in his three fast bowlers, Trueman, Statham
and Moss: no one else bowled in the innings. In the first over –
bowled by Trueman – McGlew was caught by the wicket-keeper
off his glove from a self-defensive stroke in front of his face.

There followed an attack like the body punching of a fast middle-weight boxer; an incessant, accurately directed hammering allowed no respite; the batsmen were hustled out. John Fellows-Smith was top scorer with 31 not out but at the centre of the innings, when the batsmen might have hoped the attack would be relaxed, Statham fired out Carlstein and Wesley with consecutive balls. Trueman, five for 27, Statham three for 27, Moss one for 26: South Africa were all out for 88, followed on and had one on the board when Trueman bowled Goddard.

On Saturday McGlew – unluckily run out in a regrettable, though not culpable, way – the dogged O'Linn and Waite resisted with good heart. Once more, upon the strategic cue, Statham took two wickets with consecutive balls, putting away Carlstein and – for the second time in the match, inflicting upon him the rare horror of a 'king pair' in a Test – Wesley. South Africa, all out 247, lost by eight wickets: all their twenty wickets fell to the three fast bowlers, and the rubber was won. Trueman cherished, also, going forward to catch John Waite within his crease off a normal back stroke to Alan Moss.

They were in better heart at Old Trafford and, after losing the first two days to rain, Adcock – hostile and high-bouncing – and the steady, seam-up Pothecary put out England for 260. Roy McLean played a characteristically ebullient innings of 109: Trueman and Statham took three wickets each, the off-spinner David Allen four; and South Africa were 31 behind. England batted, declared and left South Africa no time to do anything but play out a draw.

The last Test, at the Oval, deserved better than to end as a draw. Cowdrey won the toss for the fifth time in the series: England batted and Adcock and Pothecary, by a balanced blend of aggression, stamina and diligence, bowled them out for 155. The South African innings, with five scores of over 40 and no century, was 419 (Trueman and Statham three for 189 between them): a lead of 264. Cowdrey and Pullar countered with 290 for England's first wicket, and Trueman hit 16 off four balls from Pothecary before Cowdrey's declaration set South Africa an improbable 216 in three hours. Rain took away any possibility of a positive result but in the last foray McLean matched Trueman with 16 in an over off Statham and South Africa lost four wickets – two to each of the fast bowlers – for 97 before the match was left drawn.

Yorkshire won the Championship under Vic Wilson, their professional captain. They were not an outstandingly strong team; and at one point in July they played eight consecutive matches of which they won only one. Fortunately for them Lancashire, their closest competitors – who gallingly for Yorkshiremen, beat them in both 'Roses' matches – finished with a run of six matches without a win. Yorkshire had to beat Worcestershire at Harrogate in their last Championship fixture to retain the title and, despite time lost to rain and a damaged wicket, they typically rode out crisis and won by nine wickets.

Trueman was top of their bowling in aggregate and average – 132 wickets at 12.79 in only twenty-two Championship matches – and was almost as proud of a batting figure of 20.68. Neither Ryan nor Platt played regularly but he was happy in partnership for most of his county matches with Mick Cowan, back for what proved his last near-full season in the first-class game. Cowan, in the Warwickshire match at Edgbaston had a new ball spell of 10.2 overs; seven maidens; 11 runs; seven wickets: his figures for the innings were nine for 43, the best of his career.

Wilson handled Trueman intelligently, using him at starts and re-starts, taking him off before he was tired and bringing him back at any likely penetration-point. At times the procedure was varied, as at Taunton when, in their last match but one, Yorkshire stood in urgent need of points, especially since an uncertain weather outlook threatened the likelihood of a finish at Harrogate. Rain delayed the start of the Somerset match until five o'clock on Wednesday afternoon. Biddulph and Alley bowled out Yorkshire for 184 and, in a fierce attempt to gain even a first innings lead Trueman bowled twenty-seven of the sixty overs possible and took four of the five Somerset wickets that fell – the other was run out – before rain on the third day prevented any decision at all.

As well as their traditional importance, the Roses Matches of the season were crucial in the Championship. The Old Trafford fixture in August – the joint benefit match of Roy Tattersall and Malcolm Hilton – drew over 74,000 spectators on the three days. Statham – five for 43 – Ken Higgs and Tommy Greenhough put out Yorkshire for 154. Barber and Wharton reached an imposing 157 for Lancashire's second wicket, only for Trueman – four for 65 – and Ryan to batter down the rest of the innings for another 69 runs – a lead of 72. Yorkshire's 149 – Statham four for 23 – set Lancashire 78 in two hours. It seemed a practicable score but Wilson, characteristically, contested it. Trueman – fifteen overs – and Ryan – fourteen – bowled through: and when Trueman began the last over, Lancashire, with three wickets left, needed 5 to win. Clayton pushed the first ball for a single. The second comprehensively bowled Greenhough and brought in Dyson who edged his first ball past the leg stump for one. Two leg byes and a single to Clayton and the scores were level on the last ball. Trueman, realising the batsmen would run whatever happened, decided to give his wicket-keeper every chance if Dyson missed the ball, heaved himself in and bowled at the highest speed he could muster – after so long a spell – on the line of the off stump. Dyson, moving across, got an inside edge on to his pad, the ball ran for four to long leg and Lancashire had won by two wickets. It was their first double over Yorkshire in a season since 1893.

Trueman's two outstanding performances of the summer occurred in circumstances calculated to draw the highest effort from him – against Northants with Tyson, and against the old enemy, Surrey, at the Oval in Tony Lock's benefit match. At Sheffield his seven first innings wickets for 60 did not include

that of Tyson who not only made 26 (caught Close, bowled
Taylor) but countered with six for 57 (Trueman caught P. J.
Watts, bowled Tyson 12). He had, though, no answer to Trueman's seven for 65 of the second innings – making fourteen for
125, the best match-figures of his career thus far – and Yorkshire
won by six wickets. Northants found some compensation in
winning the return with a minute to spare when Brian Crump,
at the end of his conclusive stand of 169 with Raman Subba
Row, took 13 off an over from Trueman: but neither Trueman
– four wickets – nor Tyson (three) had any profound effect on
the course of the game.

Surrey's long series of Championship wins had been ill regarded in Yorkshire and to beat them in London had become
one of the side's urgent emotional needs. The Oval wicket was
placid and after Trueman bowled Stewart at 12, Parsons and
Fletcher held him up until almost lunch time. Then he crashed
through : hungry to bowl but reducing pace for the sake of
movement and with splendid catching support, he tore down
the innings to 123 with seven for 43. Yorkshire – Close a hugely
struck 198, Padgett a busy 117 – declared at 434 for four.
The resistance was sterner in the second Surrey innings: they
made 312 and Trueman had to bowl thirty-six overs of unremit-
ting aggression for such an unusual innings-proportion of
wickets and runs as seven for 82 – to better his Northants match-
figures by two runs.

At least three innings of that season gave him considerable
pleasure: against Kent at Gravesend he hit five sixes and seven
fours in 69: there were four sixes and five fours in the 52 that
halted a semi-collapse against Leicestershire at Headingley; and,
in the decisive match of the Championship with Worcestershire,
he contributed a late and hectic 56 – five sixes and three fours
– to Yorkshire's important first innings lead of 104. On the
other side of the account, that amiable character, 'Bomber'
Wells, formerly of Gloucestershire and now of Notts, hit him
for the highest six seen in modern times at Worksop – or most

other grounds – and was hilariously chastened by the infliction of a 'pair' in the return at Scarborough.

For the second year in succession Yorkshire won the Champion County's match with the Rest of England. The main contributions to this unusual achievement were the batting of Brian Bolus – 77 and 103 not out – Close and Vic Wilson, and the bowling of Trueman – six for 54 to cut open the first innings of the Rest – and Cowan (six for 89).

The next day Trueman left on a tour of South Africa and Rhodesia in an International Cavaliers team captained by Richie Benaud. This kind of exhibition cricket was not only different from, but completely foreign to, his usual non-Sunday background; but he enjoyed it; discovered that some people he had hitherto viewed with suspicion were nice enough to be his friends, and returned sunburnt and pleased with himself.

Most cricketers would be satisfied with such a season as Fred Trueman had in 1961; but it did not please him. He was seventh in the first-class bowling averages but with fewer and dearer wickets than in 1960. He played a decisive part in eight of Yorkshire's seventeen championship wins – but they lost their title to Hampshire. He won a Test Match against Australia almost single-handed and, by that performance alone, made certain that yet again he took more wickets in the series than any other English bowler; but he bowled indifferently in at least one other Test and was dropped for the fifth. He did not, when faced with the question, argue that the selectors should have picked him for the Oval: but he was deeply hurt to find that he was not in fact an automatic choice for his country.

Colin Cowdrey captained England in the first two Tests. In the draw at Edgbaston, Trueman laboured without spark to take two wickets – of Simpson and Grout – for 136 runs. At Lord's Lawry infuriated him by edging, playing and missing. He was constantly frustrated by bowling at Lawry, primarily for the reason that he regarded him, more than most, as a batsman so inferior that he ought constantly to get him out – and resented the fact that he did not. He made his point in Australia two years later, but he did not take Lawry's wicket once in the 1961 series and he found that galling, almost to the point of depression.

Australia won the Lord's Test, ultimately, because Davidson (seven for 92) and McKenzie (six for 118) were more economically effective than Trueman (six for 158) and Statham (five for 120). When Australia batted a second time needing 71 to win, the two English fast bowlers harried them to 19 for four, but could not stop them winning by five wickets. Trueman had Harvey caught at slip off a bouncer which set an uneconomic theory in his mind of that batsman's vulnerability to a short ball.

At Headingley Peter May resumed the captaincy for the first time since the second Test in West Indies, 1958-9. Les Jackson was chosen for England after a period of twelve years. It was not quite a record; as eminent a batsman as George Gunn was left out for eighteen years. He was one of the few cricketers capable of relishing such a record. In truth it should not have happened but when in August 1920 the Notts secretary handed him a letter from Lord's he put it unopened in his blazer pocket and forgot it until the following spring when he opened it to discover an invitation to go on the 1920-1 MCC tour of Australia.

The pitch, with a number of white blotches, looked peculiar before the match even started and soon proved so dusty that it was surprising to find Trueman playing the decisive part in the game rather than such spinners or cutters as Simpson, Lock, Allen, Mackay, Benaud or Illingworth. His opening overs gave him no encouragement: there was no bounce, pace or movement and, most unusually in a modern Test Match, spinners were on at both ends before one o'clock.

Lock had Lawry lbw playing no stroke, McDonald stumped by Murray and turned an off-break to O'Neill sufficiently to alarm him into caution, before Trueman and Jackson took the second new ball immediately after tea. Since the pitch had no pace, the expert observers present – and there are always plenty of them at a Headingley Test – thought spin the only profitable method of attack. The new ball was probably taken on the long accepted principle that 'it is always worthwhile' – a theory which was punctured at the cost of a Test series on the same ground three years later. Trueman proceeded to bowl as fast as he could: the pitch was slow – but two kinds of slow – slow and dead slow – and a whole sequence of batsmen playing for slow were beaten by dead slow.

Harvey made pace bowling look harmless by driving Jackson, in his first over, through the covers for four. Then O'Neill, playing too soon and confidently, edged an out-swinging half volley from Trueman to Cowdrey in the gully. At once True-man was a different – faster – bowler. He dropped one short to Harvey who turned him crisply to leg where Lock, the best backward short-leg in the world, scooped up the fast moving ball with hungry certainty. Trueman missed a caught-and-bowled from Burge who was taken in the gully off Jackson in the next over. Simpson and Mackay were lbw to Trueman and Jackson respectively. Trueman, now riding his personal and un-predictable crest, bowled Benaud, had Grout caught at the wicket and, in an hour, Australia's teatime 183 for two had become 208 for nine. As if to demonstrate the illogicality of the collapse, the last pair, Davidson and McKenzie, proceeded to make an untroubled 29 runs before May had recourse to the always likely weapon of spin and McKenzie was caught at the wicket off Allen: 237 all out.

Trueman had the figures of five for 58 which surprised most people who had seen the pitch and delighted Trueman who had latterly made some fairly crushing criticisms of the Headingley wicket: it was characteristic that he made them directly to the groundsman.

Benaud, quick to pounce on the tactical clue, used Alan Davidson – normally fast left-arm, but now at reduced pace –

to harry the England batting with spin and cut: McKenzie, too, was dangerous by virtue of his two-paced bounce. Pullar, Subba Row and Cowdrey founded the English innings by patient and watchful batting on a pitch from which the dust often rose more sharply than the ball. Trueman, sent in above his station to hit, pulled one long four and then holed out to the deep fieldsman Benaud had stationed in front of the pavilion. Lock maintained the offensive longer and England, with 299, took a lead of 62.

Jackson hit MacDonald's leg stump with a savage break-back and Australia were 13 for one at lunch but afterwards the fast bowlers gave Lawry no trouble, though May dropped the other left-hander, Harvey, off Trueman. The pattern shifted to spin at one end and, when Allen took over from Lock and had Lawry caught at the wicket from his first ball, May decided to use spin at both ends. For some time before Trueman had been talking to May, and it was clear from his gestures – like a man unlocking a door – that he wanted to try a spell of off-cutters.

May preferred the spinners and it was originally only to allow them to change ends that he brought on Trueman. The Australians in the pavilion, who could not know his purpose, observed the entry of Trueman with unease; they feared, justifiably, that in these conditions the cutter bowled at speed might turn the game. They were relieved when he bowled off his full run. Harvey, batting with all his natural grace and sensitivity went to drive the third ball of the over; it did not turn, it simply held up; the stroke was too early and Dexter made the catch at cover. That single delivery and catch tilted the match; it filled the rest of the Australian batsmen with misgivings. Trueman, with his unfailing acumen in matters relating to cricket, perceived the situation. He cut his run and, without much reduction in pace, aimed at the dust patches on and outside the right-hander's off stump. O'Neill edged an in-swinger and Cowdrey caught him at short-leg. Simpson moved across but not far enough, and was bowled. Benaud, groping, was bowled through the gate by an acute off-cutter for his second duck of the match; and the left-handed Mackay edged a catch to John Murray. In the course of twenty-seven balls Trueman had taken five wickets for no runs: Australia had collapsed from 99 for two to 109 for eight; and, as the other players stood back for him to walk in first, the Yorkshire crowd threw off its incredulity and cheered Trueman into the pavilion as they had done nine years earlier, when he struck his first destroying blow at the Indians.

After tea Jackson caught and bowled Grout; Cowdrey dived a long way at slip to catch Davidson off Trueman whose figures for the innings were six for 30: for the match, eleven for 88. England made the 59 they needed to win without appreciable difficulty and had levelled the series.

There was life in the first morning wicket at Old Trafford when Australia batted. Trueman, given his choice, began with the wind behind him from the Stretford end and in his first over he directed a ball in to the line of the leg stump, Simpson started to play a leg-glance and the out-swing was so late and sharp that before he could adjust, the ball took the back of the bat and flew through slips for four. Within the next couple of overs a catch might have been held off him at slip; and from then on it simply seemed that he did not like the match or the pitch. England had included a fresh third seam bowler – Jack Flavell of Worcestershire who came in for his first Test at the age of thirty-two – in place of Jackson; and he and Statham were sharper than Trueman. They had both hit O'Neill about the thighs – once so violently that he vomited on the pitch – before Trueman bowled him a bouncer: O'Neill shaped to hook, changed his mind, fell over and knocked off a bail: O'Neill hit wicket, bowled Trueman 11 was his only wicket of the match.

Statham – five for 53 – and Dexter – three for 16 – were mainly responsible for Australia's poor total of 190 which

seemed likely to cost them the match when England, batting well down the order, led on the first innings by 177.

Lawry – dropped at slip off Trueman when he was 25 – made a century in Australia's second innings. Trueman made one of his great short-leg catches to take him off Allen: but he did not want to bowl (his thirty-two overs cost 92 runs without a wicket). On the last morning Davidson and McKenzie, stealing a tactical march on May, put on 98 for the last wicket and that partnership altered the balance of probabilities. Before it England looked in full command, likely to need relatively few runs – 160 or so – in ample time. After it, they were under slight, though not impossible, pressure to make 256 in 230 minutes on a good batting pitch. At 150 for one, Dexter batting with glorious dominance and Subba Row solid at the other end, they were up with the clock and, again, apparently winning. Benaud bowled: as he said afterwards 'There was nothing else I could do'. He went round the wicket in the hope of pitching in the rough of Dexter's footmarks, outside the left-handed Subba Row's off stump; but it was on the offside that Dexter touched a catch to Wally Grout, the wicket-keeper. Benaud bowled May behind his legs, sweeping; had Close caught from an attempted sweep and, immediately before tea, yorked Subba Row. In less than half and hour he had bowled one of the historic spells of Test cricket to turn and win a Test and a rubber. England were 163 for five with only Barrington left of their main batting. In the tailenders' attempt to draw the match, Trueman held on for three-quarters of an hour, but Benaud (six for 70), Simpson and Davidson demolished the rest of the innings to give Australia their win by 54 runs – which meant that they retained the Ashes – with twenty minutes left.

In Yorkshire's match with the Australians Trueman, bowling at less than full pace, took one wicket – ironically that of Lawry who dragged a wide ball into his stumps – for 56; and he was not chosen for the Oval Test. Statham and Flavell were the

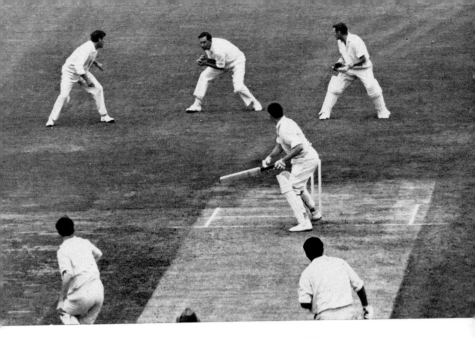

The 300th, The Oval, 1964

The Old Sweat

opening bowlers plus Dexter as reinforcement with the new ball; and an extra spinner, Tony Lock, was brought in.

It was depressingly salutary to Trueman: he had twenty wickets in four Tests and no other English bowler reached that figure in the entire series; he had taken eleven of them, though, on that dusty freak pitch at Headingley. He was dropped because he had not bowled well at Manchester; and perhaps because he seemed there to have lost his zest for bowling. This mattered deeply to him; he put a bold face on it – barely swore – but he felt his dignity as England's fast bowler affronted. It was not the first setback; would not be the last; but it was not irreversible. A devoted student of cricket records, he had an ambitious eye on his two hundredth Test wicket – he had taken 194 – and beyond to Alec Bedser's record of 236: he could not guess – and would hardly have believed it if anyone had told him – how high his ultimate figure would be.

In county cricket he was constantly effective and on his day unplayable. He could not open the bowling against Leicestershire one Saturday evening at Sheffield because he had just had a couple of teeth taken out; but he picked up the thread of the game – as fifth bowler on the Yorkshire sheet – on Monday morning with seven for 45: five for 13 in the second innings gave him the finest match figures of the year – twelve for 58. Against Derbyshire, also at Bramall Lane, he had an innings of 58 to go with a match analysis of eleven for 123. Eleven for 94 won the Essex game at Southend, but he found few pitches to suit him during the run-in to the Championship. Hampshire won the title by beating Derbyshire on the day before they met Yorkshire at Bournemouth in both counties' last match of the season. Yorkshire could not regain their title but they could demonstrate their right to it and they set about beating Hampshire as determinedly as they ever did in any match. Illingworth with twelve wickets – for 102 – was the most effective bowler but Trueman took three and, at the end, his quick thought

K

and controlled movement decided the outcome when he ran out Roy Marshall.

His self-esteem was restored in 1962. Yorkshire were again Champions; he was third in the national bowling averages – first in Yorkshire's – and firmly reinstated in the England team. Although he was again left out of the Oval Test, this time, in company with other established players, he was 'rested' to give younger men a chance before the Australian tour; and, with the rubber won, to avoid handicapping counties involved in the final stages of the Championship.

The Test series with Pakistan was settled all too quickly and easily when England won the first three Tests – two by an innings and one by nine wickets – and, to most Yorkshire players at least, the Championship, especially since they won in the centenary year of the county club, was of greater significance.

Trueman performed his now invariable highly efficient job for the county in his benefit season. He chose the match with Surrey, at Sheffield – the county ground nearest to Maltby, and where he had enjoyed some of his finest bowling spells – and although rain and bad light cut playing time and led to a draw, the fund raised £9,331, less than £500 short of Len Hutton's record for a Yorkshire benefit.

He was nowadays a senior, and a weapon to be kept sharp; hence he was excused the two away games with Oxford and Cambridge Universities; and, in a strange way, he missed them. Representative matches primarily dictated that he played in only twenty-three of the county's thirty-two Championship fixtures of which they won fourteen – only two of them without him: and he had a decisive effect on eight of the remaining twelve. His second innings five for 29 defeated Lancashire – who had led on the first innings – in the Whitsun Roses Match. His regular victims, Notts, suffered again – losing eight for 84 to him in the first innings, two for 58 in the second.

In this period Yorkshire and Hampshire played some absorbing matches; none more surprising than at Bradford in

1962. Yorkshire, taking first innings, never established themselves against Shackleton who bowled through the entire innings – thirty-one overs – to take seven for 78. Trueman – five
for 34 – similarly troubled Hampshire and only Henry Horton
(67), who always played Trueman resolutely, lifted them to
165 and a lead of 14. Again Shackleton bowled through the
innings and Yorkshire were 70 for six when Trueman came in
to Wilson and hit Shackleton furiously back over his head to
the football stand in a partnership of 67. Hampshire, wanting
163 to win actually reached 156 for five – seven short with five
wickets left – when Trueman, who had not taken a wicket in
the innings, took the ball, had Jim Gray – top scorer for Hampshire with 78 – caught at the wicket and, with Illingworth,
cleaned up the innings for only one more run, to give Yorkshire an amazing win by five runs.

It was too much to expect that such an otherwise unstressed
season could pass for him without some incident. He became an
historic figure by captaining the Players in the last Gentlemen
v. Players match at Lord's. After it ended he took part in a
television programme and it was half-past-nine before he and
Phil Sharpe – who had also played at Lord's – set off for
Taunton where Yorkshire were to meet Somerset the next day.
As one would expect on a Friday night in July, the road from
London to the West was choked. They made slow progress and
– as it is easy to do – he missed the right fork west of Spark-
ford and went on almost to Exeter before he realised his mistake
and turned back. They did not reach the team's hotel at
Taunton until half past two in the morning.

They wrote their morning call times on the hotel board and
went to bed. Trueman did not go to the room allotted to him
in the book – nor the one for which he had booked a call – and
consequently no one called him next morning. He has been a
late sleeper all his days and he had already been warned by his
captain that the next time he did not meet the county orders –
to be on the ground an hour before the start of the first day,

half an hour on the second and third – he would be left out of the side.

Warnings do not make heavy sleepers wake early. Phil Sharpe, who waited downstairs for him until twenty-past-ten had tried to locate him, only to find his allocated room empty. Enquiries short of the level that might cause embarrassment did not discover him in time to be on the ground, according to orders, by half past ten: and Sharpe left the hotel to report on time. Trueman woke a few minutes afterwards, shaved, dressed and reached the dressing-room at eleven o'clock to be told by Vic Wilson that he had already announced the Yorkshire team – without Trueman – and had informed the press that he had dropped him for failing to report on time. It is not surprising if the steady, quiet Wilson had become irked by three seasons of dealing with the restless Trueman. This, though, was pure sergeant-major. Trueman in the past had generally been successful at Taunton and on this occasion Yorkshire did not take a single point from the game (Somerset took first innings lead in a drawn match). That result might have cost them the Championship – there were only four points between Yorkshire and Worcestershire at the end. Sharpe had, too, already told Wilson that Fred had arrived – and arrived extremely late – the night before. A telephone call to the hotel could have roused him and it is hard not to assume that the opportunity to punish was welcomed, perhaps on a 'discipline is discipline' basis.

Trueman was sent back to Yorkshire to appear before the county club's disciplinary committee with instructions that, if he was not picked for the Trent Bridge Test – due to start on the following Thursday – he was to rejoin the team on Tuesday night at Bristol for the remaining match of what Yorkshire used to call their 'Western Tour'.

Wilson was a strong man to create such a situation; he had to be stronger still to sustain it: he was raked with a mixture of opprobrium, sarcasm, reason and straight curses enough to quell most people. There was no need to announce the team at a quarter to eleven. You knew I was here – got in late and should probably sleep in. What? Drive 400 miles to Yorkshire and 400 miles back to Bristol, when it is only fifty miles away? How bloody daft can you get? Where the hell are the press chaps? – all luridly sprinkled. Nevertheless, when the steam had been let off Trueman set off for Yorkshire. On Monday Sir William Worsley (President of the county club), Brian Sellers (Chairman of the Cricket committee) and John Nash (secretary), not exactly, as the defendant remarked, 'Fred's Fan Club' heard the case. Vic Wilson's report was before them. Trueman told his story. Had he refused to report to Bristol? That did not arise, he argued, he had since been picked to play in the Test at that time. He was given his car-travel allowance to the meeting, the price of a lunch and his match fee was sanctioned for the game at Taunton. He felt, with understandably malicious glee, that he had stuffed someone – or everyone – and went off to the Test well satisfied.

Vic Wilson decided to retire at the end of this season. He had done an honest job. In the three years of his captaincy Yorkshire had been Champions twice and runners-up once: he had taken some magnificent catches at short-leg – not least off Trueman, whose bowling he directed sympathetically and effectively – and within his technical limitations he had batted well. It was decided to make a presentation to mark his performance and his retirement. Fred Trueman, approached for a subscription reacted predictibly – 'What, for him? What? That bugger who sent me home from Taunton? – not bloody likely'. Ronnie Burnet diplomatically persuaded Mrs Trueman to contribute to the fund: but Fred made it clearly known that he had not departed from his original decision.

A one-sided Test series brought him some statistical satisfaction. When England made 544 for five declared in the first Test – at Edgbaston – Pakistan were at a disadvantage they never made good : Statham with six wickets, Trueman four, did all that was needed of them: the spinners Allen and Lock shared the other ten and Pakistan lost by an innings.

Statham was injured and replaced by Coldwell at Lord's where on a green wicket, Pakistan, given the doubtful pleasure of batting first, revealed a marked distaste for pace bowling in English conditions. Trueman, never slow to detect and probe such a sore spot, wielded late and sharp swing and made his shorter ball rear unpleasantly enough to induce a self-destructive split-mindedness in the batsmen who faced him. He had the wickets of Hanif – 'the little master' – Burki – his two hundredth Test wicket – and Mushtaq: Coldwell and Dexter dealt with Imtiaz, Saeed and Alim, and Pakistan were 76 for six at lunch. The last four wickets made another 24; Trueman – six for 31 – and Coldwell swept them aside. Another long innings – of 153 – by Tom Graveney helped England to a lead of 270. On a pitch of milder pace Burki and Nasim made hundreds in the second Pakistani innings: the bowlers had to work harder, and Coldwell took six wickets to Trueman's three.

Another innings win at Headingley – Statham six wickets, Trueman four – decided the rubber. Rain reduced the Trent Bridge Test by more than a day and Pakistan, through some determined batting by Mushtaq, hung on for a draw – Trueman five wickets, Statham four. Neither was needed at the Oval: they were already on the sailing list for the winter tour of Australia.

The 1962-3 tour of Australia was, like that of 1958-9, a disappointment both to England and to the people who watched it. The MCC team, captained by Ted Dexter, was managed – as the result of a casual domestic joke – by the Duke of Norfolk. It was an odd appointment. He could not, of course, carry out the manager's duties for the entire tour, which necessitated sending out S. C. Griffith, secretary of MCC to take his place while he went home to attend to 'private duties'. His influence delighted a few Australians; but displeased more of both countries, including Fred Trueman, who found his antipathy justified.

He did nothing better on the tour than his three for 83 and five for 62 which, with the batting of Sheppard, Dexter and Cowdrey, gave England the second Melbourne Test, their only win of the series. David Sheppard described his series of stints from the bottom end as the finest sustained and accurate fast bowling he had ever seen. His four for 60 represented England's strongest bid to win the eventually drawn Adelaide match. To his immense pleasure he took Lawry's wicket once in each Test.

He probably should not have played in the first Test. He had trouble with a displaced bone at the base of the spine and was still being given pain-killing injections when play began. Before the match it was reported that Australian specialists had discovered he had such a serious congenital spinal weakness that he should be sent home for surgical treatment and might well never bowl again. Journalists in England interviewed his father who said the story was 'bloody daft': and he was proved right.

With twenty wickets at 26.05, he was second in the bowling averages of the Australian Test to Allen and – by one – in aggregate to Titmus. In first-class matches of the complete tour he took more wickets than anyone else and only Fred Titmus bowled more overs.

Three remarks from this tour have gone down in the Trueman annals. In the two days while the party, flown out to Aden, waited for their boat to Australia – the *Canberra* – they were generously entertained. At one party a local Sheikh was present and one of the hosts pointed him out and said 'He's got a hundred-and-ninety-six wives'. 'Has he?' said Fred. 'Does he know that with another four he could have a new ball?'

David Sheppard who had interrupted a clerical career to make the tour, scored an important century at Melbourne but otherwise did not distinguish himself and, after a long absence from the first-class game, he not unexpectedly dropped a number of catches. After one miss Fred, the injured bowler, said, 'Kid yourself it's Sunday, Rev., and keep your hands together'. Sheppard maintained close relations with clerical circles in Australia and on one occasion presented the MCC team to the Bishop of Perth, after which Fred with a jerk of the head remarked 'I suppose he's your senior pro?'

Impressed by the pre-tour lunch with its exhortations to the players' responsibilities to be 'ambassadors as well as cricketers', Fred, as anyone who knew him would have foreseen, did his naïve damnedest – even if he was not convinced of the validity of the briefing. Struggling past some rebukes by His Grace – 'call me Dukie' – for occurrences he did not even recognise, he set out his stall. In Perth he assured the social questioners that their lager was as fine as anything he had ever drunk in Europe – 'And I've been to Germany, too': at Adelaide he admired the South Australian wines with vast unfounded authority: at Melbourne he agreed that the Melbourne Cricket Ground was the finest sports arena in the world. By the time he reached Sydney the veneer of diplomacy was wearing thin. What did he think of 'our bridge'? 'Your bridge? *Our* bloody bridge you should say – bugger it – a Yorkshire firm – Dorman and Long – built it – and you bastards still ain't paid for it'. The Duke marked that one against him in the book.

This had obviously to be the last tour either Trueman or Statham would ever make to Australia; and the composition of the team ensured that they would have much work to do though they were both – one before the tour and the other on it – thirty-two years old, and over the reputed hill of fast bowlers. Trueman gained more genuine respect from the rest of the party on this tour than on any before. He could still deal the blistering retort – 'repartee you know' – curse a non-trier or an edger; pull out cold on the rest of the party and spend the evening alone. Against that, his heart – at least his cricketing heart – showed through the flesh. He wanted savagely to succeed, to bowl out more and more batsmen. Statham, Graveney,

Allen and Pullar went home after the Australian part of the tour: Trueman went on to New Zealand where, having, like Statham, passed in Australia Alec Bedser's record of 236 Test wickets, he pulled ahead to 250.

CHAPTER TWELVE

The Burn-up

To watch the twenty cricketing years of Fred Trueman was to be perpetually amazed not merely at his physical self-renewal which alone was quite phenomenal but also, by his capacity, when it seemed that he had reached his peak, to attain a new degree of stature, almost a new dimension of ability.

When he came back from the Dexter tour of Australia he was weary: he was thirty-two – eight months younger than Brian Statham whom the critics thought had begun to wilt in Australia. Statham, too, was entitled to be tired: for thirteen years he had driven a by no means mighty body into a blend of sustained accuracy, hostility and stamina barely matched in the history of cricket; indeed, but for Trueman, we should call him unique; and he had still in hand a final killing volley to be fired after Trueman had gone. Now, though, he could no longer sustain his former penetration through a five-day Test on a slow pitch; and, at heart, he did not want to.

Trueman did: and, partly because of his greater physical strength, but basically because of his burning hunger for the glory of fast bowling achievement, he forced himself ahead of the essentially relaxed and amiable 'George'. He was due to burn out: instead, in the summer of 1963, he blazed up like a smouldering fire fed with a handful of dry brushwood.

Those who knew him perceived at once the reason for Trueman's blaze of 1963 in the presence of the West Indian opening bowlers, Hall and Griffith. Wesley Hall was the latest holder of the title 'fastest bowler in the world' which was alone sufficient

to hoist Trueman to heights of bellicose contention. A thread
of genuine mutual respect, however, ran through the intense
competition between these two. They both – usually – honoured
the conventions of the fast bowlers' union, so that (except at
Lord's in 1963) Trueman could constantly play Hall off the
front foot when more distinguished batsmen – non-union members – would have done so only at peril of a bouncer between
the eyes. Hall, for his part, in the Headingley Test of 1963,
drove Trueman straight for one of the few sixes ever hit off
him. Griffith was the reputedly deadly dealer of bouncers and
yorkers and, without comment on the fairness or otherwise of
his delivery, it was Trueman's constant aim to demonstrate his
own superiority in this traffic. All his career he was in contention; not only with opposing batsmen, but with other fast
bowlers. Like Lock, he regarded his bowling partner as a rival,
to be bested at all cost. As to the fast bowlers of the other side,
they were doubly opponents. It is perhaps one of the most
remarkable facets of 'George' Statham's personality that Fred
did not hate his guts.

He may have been ageing in 1963 but every time he went on
a Test match field – and once, provocatively, before that – he
felt the aggravation of Hall and Griffith and responded to it with
blazing spirit.

Domestically, the appointment of Brian Close as captain of
Yorkshire met with Fred Trueman's approval. They were, it
may be said with more accuracy than is at once apparent, old
sparring partners. Neither hesitated to give the other the full
blast of his opinion, whether favourable or not; they were blunt
– or sharp – speakers with genuine respect for one another's
cricketing ability.

The Yorkshire team was gradually being reshaped. During
this season, Platt faded out of the side; Cowan did not play at
all; Ryan kept going and, with the newcomer Tony Nicholson
– medium-pace swing – gave Trueman new ball assistance: but,
once more, he carried the main burden of the pace bowling.

Illingworth and Don Wilson bowled off-spin and slow left-arm competently enough for most opponents while, on the batting side, Geoff Boycott moved into the side like a cat stepping into an armchair; spread himself with a century in each of the Roses matches and settled into residence for life.

Trueman tuned up with some hard work in the batsmen's match, MCC v Yorkshire, when 777 runs were scored and only ten wickets fell; and against Cambridge University when he took four for 44 and hit a self-satisfied 49. At Northampton he scored the first century of his career – 104 – and, when wickets were needed to win the match on the third afternoon, he took three quickly. The Kent match was unremarkable: then, with quite savage sustained and accurate hostility – rested for only one over in the two innings – he took four for 18 and six for 18 in the innings win over Warwickshire. At Middlesbrough, hackles up against the West Indians, he took five for 38 in their first innings, five for 33 in the second; scored 55 and 20 not out, made two short leg catches: and Yorkshire beat the touring side by 111 runs. Next morning at Bradford he bowled out Gloucestershire for 80 – only Arthur Milton reached double figures – and, with eight for 45 and almost a fortnight of May to run, he had taken 39 wickets for 333 runs – an average of less than nine – an amazing spring.

The following day was Sunday, Trueman himself was, under the terms of his contract, precluded from reporting anything about the recent Australian tour until a year had elapsed. However, the newspaper that published his column – *The People* – reported information from 'a close friend' that Lord's had stopped £50 of his £150 good conduct bonus for the trip and that he regarded this as such an 'insult' that he refused ever to play for England again. He had been in the sporting headlines for a fortnight; now he almost leapt off the front page. In sharp contrast to his reaction in 1954, when he was grateful that his journalist friend did not publish his similar avowal, this time he was fully prepared – all but happy – to stand by it, or even repeat it. The circumstances, of course, were different. If Trueman had given the selectors such an ultimatum in 1954 when four or five alternative choices were available to them, they would certainly have stood on their dignity, and taken him at his word: he might have spent long out of the England team. Now, however, they could not do without him: and he knew it. He did not lose by the revelation, for admirers in Australia – where his clowning, forthrightness and bowling made him widely popular – sent him cheques for far more than the deducted £50.

Illingworth, also mulcted of £50, was less fortunate: and neither ever received any satisfaction as to why they had been fined. MCC made a statement that the decision had been taken by a committee of MCC acting on reports and advice from Ted Dexter, the captain, and the Duke of Norfolk, manager of the touring team. Demands for a hearing or a discussion were refused: the Duke proved extremely evasive and the punishment – without a hearing – rankled with both men for many years.

Singularly unworried by his apparent self-immolation, Fred Trueman passed from the washed-out Gloucestershire match to one with Hampshire at Leeds. Although he took only four wickets, his 37 – run out – was the highest score but one of Yorkshire's second innings. It was played doggedly, on the third afternoon, in an attempt to draw the match and avoid a Yorkshire defeat. As time grew short, Peter Sainsbury tossed his slow left-arm higher and higher in the attempt to persuade him into an injudicious stroke. Fred, resolutely abjuring his big swing, pushed forward with puritanical rectitude. Sainsbury raised the curve even more alluringly; Trueman continued with his defensive prod. Eventually he turned to Leo Harrison, the wicket-keeper, with 'My word he chucks it up, this cock, doesn't he? I'm all right when his arm comes over, but I'm out of form by the time the bloody ball gets here.' Later Sainsbury, unsuccessful, went off for Shackleton and Ingleby-Mackenzie pushed the close fieldsmen up around the bat. Fred surveyed them with some asperity and the words, 'Stand back, go on, stand back – or I'll appeal against the light'.

Before the team was chosen for the first West Indian Test of 1963, Willie Watson, a member of the selection committee carefully chosen and primed, went to see Fred with a diplomatic brief to suffer the oaths and ensure that he withdrew his ultimatum. Accordingly, four days before the team for the first Test was to be announced, MCC, in a unilateral statement, informed the world that 'F. S. Trueman has decided to accept the decision of MCC with regard to the bonus for the recent MCC tour of Australia and so far as he and MCC are concerned the matter is closed'. He had cocked yet another snook at authority – this time the gilded dome of the establishment – and they had come to him and asked him to relent. He flexed his biceps, looked ahead down the years when a fast bowler was supposed to be finished and – not widely but measurably – relaxed more than he had ever done before in his cricketing career. There was only one disturbing item of uncertainty: Lord's had not paid up the £50: had they had the last laugh?

He made a generally quiet way to the Test at Old Trafford, except that, on the preceding Saturday morning, at Bramall Lane he contributed three of the wickets to Lancashire's dilemma of 28 for five. The Test always looked likely to go with the toss which Worrell won: and West Indies batted on just such another slow, true wicket as had disheartened Trueman in the previous year. This time he maintained sense and control, bowling defensively, mainly outside the off stump – especially to Sobers – through a West Indian total of 501 for six declared. Both Carew (16) and Worrell (74 not out) were dropped off him; he, for his part, missed Hunte (182) at short-leg when he had made 66. Forty overs and two for 95 was the measure of his work. The other pace bowlers did little better – that was what mattered to him – even in two England innings, Hall had only three for 90, Griffith one for 48, while Statham – o for 121 – and Dexter – o for 16 – emphasised that the pitch had deteriorated from plumb to a slow turner. Gibbs – eleven wickets in the match – and Sobers – bowling spinners – put out England twice and West Indies, clearly the better-equipped side, won by ten wickets with more than a day in hand.

Statham's poor match – apart from one fierce unlucky over with the second new ball – cost him his place. Derek Shackleton of Hampshire, eleven years after his previous Test and now thirty-eight, came back to open the bowling opposite Trueman at Lord's with his accurate medium-paced swing. He was recalled for two reasons. The first was his remarkable record of success at Lord's over many years; and also because it was thought that the West Indian batsmen, rarely disconcerted by great pace, to which they were accustomed in their domestic game, were vulnerable to the greater degree of movement – through the air and off the pitch – of the English fast-medium or medium-paced bowler in his own home conditions.

Again Dexter lost the toss; rain delayed the start half an hour. Trueman bowled the opening over and Conrad Hunte took three fours – only one deliberate – and a single off the first four balls. Then he and Shackleton dropped into a groove, using every scrap of greenness in the wicket. Shackleton, in particular, moved the ball so bewilderingly in the air and off the pitch on the first morning that the early West Indies batsmen were uncharacteristically subdued. Three chances were missed off Shackleton; another half dozen edges from both bowlers might have gone to hand for all the batsmen knew; West Indies had only 47 by lunch but were happily surprised not to have lost a wicket.

Dexter's tactical plan seemed simply to be containing with Shackleton while Trueman struck at the other end. They bowled seventy-two overs between them in the day, and held West Indies to 245 for six. Trueman took five of those six. It was one of his shaggy days; the humidity that made his out-swinger 'go' so late also pumped the sweat through his heavy undervest to darken his shirt with the ancient stain of labour. His forelock,

jerked forward by the delivery-heave, clung moistly to his forehead: he crouched at short leg with a trouser leg rucked
damply on his calf and, when the other players stood back
for him to walk in first at the close of play, his face was
sheeny grey with exhaustion: and he dragged his head back to
return a friendly jeer with the effort of a drained man, getting
back to his seat in the dressing room on will-power.

Shackleton, who had no wickets on the first day, took the
last three on the second morning. Trueman finished with six
for 100 from forty-four overs: West Indies 301 all out.

Dexter – at his most splendidly imperious – Barrington and
Titmus, in their contrasted fashions, made the chief contributions to England's 297 – only four behind on the first innings –
but Griffith's five for 91 was the goad for Trueman. On Saturday, with gates at Lord's closed on a tensely gripped crowd,
Hunte had the effrontery to pull him for six before he nicked
Shackleton to slip and, at 15 for two; 64 for three, 84 for four,
104 for five, the England bowlers, Trueman – especially –
Shackleton and Allen were taking the game. Trueman fired ball
after ball through Sobers, whom he had treated with such wary
respect at Old Trafford. A century by Butcher with support
from Worrell, steadied the innings temporarily until, on Monday morning, Trueman, in precisely directed fury, and Shackleton, knocked down the last five wickets in less than half an hour
for fifteen runs. They had carried out their operation according
to plan.

	Overs	Maidens	Runs	Wickets
Trueman	26	9	52	5
Shackleton	34	14	72	4

Trueman's analysis was the best achieved by any pace bowler
in the match and he walked off, arms and legs truculently
bowed – and satisfied. England wanted 234 to win; 118 with
seven wickets left. When bad light ended the fourth day's play
they had made 116 for three – in effect for four, because

Cowdrey, batting as well as he had done for a long time, had his left forearm broken by a ball from Hall that reared up in a twilight that made fast bowling unsafe.

It was an afternoon of gripping tensions and of climaxes which would have seemed far-fetched if a playwright had created them, but which were the outcome of finest effort by some unmistakably great cricketers. Hall bowled all the afternoon at such pace as, it has been said, he was never able to produce again. When the invaluable Barrington was prised out, Close maintained the attempt in an innings of characteristic courage and an equally characteristic end. Parks made a couple of bold and handsome strokes: Titmus hung on. One ball was enough for Trueman: the fast bowlers' union was forgotten, he fended off a lifter from Hall in front of his face and Deryck Murray made the catch. All rested on Close, and his 70 – by far his best Test score in England until then – put England within sight of winning. Then he decided to charge the West Indies paring inevitable at this stage of the match – Hall and Griffith – and hit two fours before he edged Griffith to Murray. England, with twenty minutes left, needed fifteen to win. When Wesley Hall – who had bowled ever since the afternoon start – began the last over, all four results were possible. There could not be another over and Worrell strolled across to Hall, and said, with a cold half-smile – 'If you bowl a no-ball I'll kill you'.

Hall gathered himself, and without a sign of the weariness which must have flooded his body, bounded into the surging, savage rhythm of the most stirring run-up in modern cricket, and bowled with the calm control of a fresh bowler on an ordinary afternoon. It was not ordinary. This was one of those rare occasions when, at the highest level of performance and with much at stake, the competitive elements of cricket – runs, wickets and time – fuse into a dramatic unity. The odds were on the bowler; but two edged strokes. . . .

All those who were there – and because of television they

L

were millions – will recall that over of high drama – six balls to go; eight runs to get; two wickets to fall; only Cowdrey – already padded up and practising one-handed strokes in the dressing-room – to come.

Six times the crowd hushed; six times burst again into babble; Shackleton swung at the first ball and missed; he dabbed at the second, ran, and both batsmen got home for the single; Allen glanced the third for one; with Allen already backing up, Shackleton missed the fourth, overbalanced and was run out. two final balls were straight; Allen played meticulously back to the first one, forward to the other and the most tense of Test Matches was over. Men on both sides – not least Trueman – had done enough to win it; but it was better left thus prodigiously drawn. The injured Cowdrey drew it by coming back.

Lord's created a public for the series, only for appalling weather to virtually halve playing time in the first three days at Edgbaston. Heavy overnight rain delayed the start. Dexter won the toss – when he would happily have left the decision to Worrell – and, after contemplating putting West Indies in, took first innings. The wicket – wet underneath – was too soft for Hall, who could find no bounce in it but Sobers – five for 60 – curving the ball through the damp air, hinted at the possibilities for the English bowlers. Only Brian Close (55) and Mick Stewart (39) scored more than 30 as England made an anxious way to 216 by the end of Friday. The Edgbaston gates were closed on a 28,000 Saturday crowd when rain allowed no play until ten-to-one and none after tea. In that time West Indies lost four men – the first two to a baulked and obviously indignant Trueman – for 110.

So, when play began again on Monday morning two-thirds of the time was gone and five-eighths of the wickets remained; few could have expected a result on a wicket that had rolled out true and firmer than on any previous day. Certainly no one anticipated that the six remaining West Indies wickets – including those of Butcher, Sobers and Worrell – would go down before lunch – in fact in about an hour and a quarter – for 76 runs. Dexter and Trueman shared them, Trueman, cutting his run and his speed, intent on getting his left shoulder even further round, made the ball move late off an immaculate length and line. His two keenest blows were those that put out Butcher and Sobers – right-hand and left – each beaten by a ball that struck back : Butcher was lbw, Sobers bowled by a ball pushed across him which amazingly pitched wide of his off stump and hit the middle. Murray and Hall made a stand while Trueman rested; Dexter called him back and he took the last two wickets in consecutive overs. West Indies, 186, were thirty runs behind on the first innings – Trueman five for 75 – and still the probability was of a draw.

England did their best to push the score along. Dexter in partnership with Philip Sharpe – playing in his first Test – grew from caution to command and in his final foray, struck Worrell for five fours, before he was stumped by Murray when England were exactly 200 ahead. An overnight partnership between Sharpe – highest scorer of the match with 85 not out – and Lock put on 89 and, when Lock was bowled by Gibbs, Dexter declared and asked West Indies to score 309 in 280 minutes.

Shackleton and Trueman made them 10 for two; they still pressed for a win: Dexter bowled Butcher, and at lunch they were 51 for three.

In less than an hour afterwards Trueman took six of the seven remaining West Indian wickets. This was cold, objective, knowledgeable killing: even the dropped catch did not matter. He was in his element, certain that no batsman could live in it: yet less than two hours earlier Hall, Griffith and Sobers – seam up – had bowled there with no effect. The bouncer was solely a tactical weapon – twice in the match it brought him a wicket when it was bowled at the strategically correct moment. For the rest he hammered the ball into a responsive wicket with all the experience of his career. He came up his shortened run, head rock-steady, the arm cut over high : his body seemed to shudder at the thud of his left foot into the ground and he made the ball move away from the right-hander's bat at speed far too great for any batsman to survive for long. He had seven men up, plus the wicket-keeper and he did not bowl a bad ball. He took the last six wickets in twenty-four balls in which there was only one stroke – a nick for four by Gibbs who was amusedly not out. England had won by 217 runs and levelled the series. Trueman, seven for 44 in the last innings, twelve for 119 in the match, had now taken 25 wickets in the first three games of the series.

At Headingley West Indies again won the toss and batted first on a firm wicket in good weather. In those conditions they were always likely to win through their long batting – Worrell went in at number eight – all-round ability and variety of bowling. England's batting was uncertain, and their bowling – on good pitches – not sufficiently penetrative. Trueman and Shackleton took an early wicket apiece in the first innings when Trueman, who lopped off the tail, bowled forty-six overs – more than anyone else in any innings of the match. A century by Sobers was the core of the West Indies total of 397: England's 174 – only as high as that by grace of an impressive 53 by Lock at number nine – made the result inevitable. Trueman bowled Hunte for 4 and had McMorris lbw for 1 at the start of the second West Indian innings but the eventual asking price of 453 was far beyond England's powers or hopes.

Statham was brought back for the Oval to form, with Trueman, Shackleton and Dexter, a seam attack relieved only by Lock. England went in first on a superb batting wicket, everyone except Sharpe (63) seemed 'in' and then was out: 275 did not seem enough for their purpose. The West Indies batsmen, apart from Hunte and Butcher, were unduly diffident on such a generous stage. Trueman and Statham took three wickets each, there were two run-outs and England found themselves with a first innings lead of 29. This time Sharpe made 83 of an otherwise indifferent England 223. Nevertheless it gave them an outside chance of winning – and squaring the series – through their pace bowling, on a pitch where Hall, Griffith and Sobers in his faster fashion had proved so effective that Worrell used Gibbs for only nine overs in the second innings. The final irony was that Trueman, who had earlier turned his left ankle in an old foothold, did not bowl on Saturday evening, had treatment on Sunday, and on Monday sent down one over before he limped off and did not appear again. He had a combination of strained ligaments and bruised heel which put him out of action for ten days. His departure weakened the England out-cricket psychologically as well as technically and, carefully steered by Hunte – 108 not out – West Indies came safely to take the match by eight wickets, and the rubber by three to one.

Statistically this was Fred Trueman's best season; he was top of the Test, first-class and Yorkshire bowling averages. For England he took thirty-four wickets at 17.47; Dexter was second with seven at 32.42; and Shackleton – 15 – was the only other bowler to take more than seven wickets. In the first-class table he had 129 at 15.15: and, in sixteen of the matches that won Yorkshire the Championship once more, seventy-six at 12.8, an average two lower than the second man. At Bradford in August he performed his fourth hat-trick – and his third against Notts – when he took the wickets of Millman, Davison and Wells. As well as the three hat-tricks, he five times took two wickets with consecutive balls against Notts; on three occasions Maurice Hill faced, and survived, the third ball.

His century against Northants in May seemed strangely to affect his batting until the end of the season. He became more correct – and could, indeed, be suspected of putting on 'style' – but less successful than formerly. Happily at Scarborough, for an England XI against Young England – his first game after his injury at the Oval – he reverted to type and scored a hundred in sixty-seven minutes which turned and won the match. He hit six sixes and eleven fours and made his century while his partner, Trevor Bailey, scored 19. With 50 and 33 for T. N. Pearce's XI against the West Indians he finished the Scarborough Festival full of explosive conviviality and talk.

CHAPTER THIRTEEN

The Broken Record

Those who live by statistics must die by statistics and, by the standard of figures, the season of 1964 was for Fred Trueman one of the high peaks and an unusual number of troughs. In five more Championship matches for Yorkshire than in 1963 he took nine fewer wickets at an average almost eight runs higher – and that alone accounted for the county's fall to fifth in the table. For England he was top of the bowling against Australia in both aggregate and average: and he passed the record on which he had fixed his aim – 300 wickets in Test cricket.

He came out of the rain-ruined Trent Bridge Test with three wickets and what should have been an effective chastening. He had long been convinced – with some justification – that O'Neill was vulnerable to the bouncer. When Dexter's fifth day declaration set Australia 242 to win, he proceeded to ply him with short-pitched stuff and O'Neill hooked four consecutive balls for boundaries. Rain, which almost halved the due playing time, put an early end to the matter.

More rain washed out all play on the first two days at Lord's and, when Australia batted in damp, English-type conditions, Trueman, with calm control, bowling straight, let the seam do its work and earned himself five for 48. The match never approached a finish.

Headingley was a costly match for England, remains a controversial one, and was the most unrelievedly disastrous of Trueman's career. England took first innings and made an unimpressive 268. Australia, after being 124 for one, were reduced to 178 for seven by the spin of Norman Gifford and Fred Titmus who induced such anxious uncertainty in the batting that the score barely moved for almost an hour. Only Peter Burge – a most Australian Australian – remained of the main batsmen and he was uneasy, failing to 'middle' the ball. His sole support consisted of the tail – Hawke, who was already with him – Grout and Corling. England were in a dominant position. At 187 the new ball became available and, to the surprise of one school of thought – which would keep on bowlers who are doing well – Dexter took it, and gave it to Trueman and Flavell to finish off the innings, as Trueman at his best would certainly have done.

Instead he sacrificed the match to his theory that Burge was an uncertain hooker. On a fast wicket he might have proved it: here he was discredited. He loosened up and took the new ball against Hawke who scored a single. Then came this incredible series of medium-paced long hops which rose in a simple arc and, in what must have seemed like a bowler's nightmare, Burge – always happier against pace than spin – hooked him with murderous ease. A four in the next new ball over (to Hawke): 21424 Hawke, 3, Burge 10 – in the third: two fours to Burge in the fourth (25 off three overs). Flavell did no better, 41 runs (Burge 29, Hawke 12) came in seven overs (40 in six) of the new ball. Dexter took them both off, but it was too late: the match had been tilted. Soon Hawke, too, was playing pace and then spin with impunity: the entire balance and feeling of the game had changed. Australia were winning. Burge reached his century before Hawke – his partner in a stand of 105 – was caught at slip off Trueman: Australia were 283 for eight at the close of play. Next morning Grout came out with Burge; again Trueman bowled short; Grout hooked him for three fours and his first two overs cost fourteen runs. He eventually had Burge startlingly caught (off a hook) by the substitute – Alan Rees of Glamorgan – but by then the last three Australian wickets had put on 212 runs; the game, and, as it proved, the rubber, had been decided. An elder player of the county shook his head in sad disbelief: 'Trueman bowled Bad' he said. A Yorkshireman can offer no sterner condemnation. Australia won by seven wickets.

Not surprisingly, Trueman was left out of the England team for the Old Trafford Test, and was fortunate not to be dropped permanently – as he could well have been if another pace-bowler had succeeded at Manchester – for several of the selectors took an extremely unfavourable view of his non-effort at Headingley. So, although the announcement of his omission induced a fierce attack of injured pride, decorated with indignation, he cannot have been sorry, in the end, to have missed that monumentally boring display of batting gluttony in which 1,281 runs were scored and only nineteen wickets fell. He could hardly have done better than in his two previous – extremely ordinary-performances on that lifeless strip. On the other hand, his replacement, Fred Rumsey – two for 99 – did not survive to the Oval, so Trueman came back.

England had another poor first innings of 182 – and Trueman, quite unable to match the effect of McKenzie and Hawke for Australia, had bowled twenty-six overs for 80 runs and no wicket a few minutes before lunch on Saturday, when he saw Ted Dexter, in one of his glazed moods, with the ball in his hand. 'Give it me,' he said and put himself on at the pavillion end. His fifth ball bowled Ian Redpath; Graham McKenzie touched the sixth – an out-swinger – to Cowdrey at slip. There was no time for more; the players went in to lunch. So, by the dramatic chance which coloured so much of his life, he went in to lunch leaving a large Oval crowd and a vast Saturday television and radio audience to share his forty minutes of suspense. He was 'on' a hat trick for his three-hundredth Test wicket – a figure no one else had ever reached.

Before he touched the ball again he had created an unrecordable record by bringing all the spectators at the Oval back from lunch to their seats for the restart of play. Cartwright duly bowled the overture: Dexter called up an umbrella field and Trueman, with appropriate dramatic pauses, considered, limbered, set off – and bowled wide of Hawke's off stump. He bowled until the new ball was available – with its horrid echoes of Headingley – and then found the edge of Hawke's bat with a late out-swinger and once again Colin Cowdrey at slip made the catch. That was the statistically important achievement: not one thousandth as significant as that of Burge would have been on the second afternoon at Headingley, but cheered and back slapped because it was the three-hundredth.

Asked whether he thought anyone would ever equal his record he quoted George Hirst who, asked the same question after he had taken 200 wickets and scored 2,000 runs in the season of 1906 said 'If he does he will be tired': Trueman made it 'bloody tired'.

He had Corling, also caught at slip, to end the first Australian innings; rain prevented a second, made the match a draw and left the series, as well as the Ashes, with Australia.

To his chagrin he was not chosen for the winter tour of South Africa. There was a good case for not taking him. The selection committee conferred with observers in Yorkshire on the basis of his county form and considered in Tests, an indifferent and tactically imprudent performance at Trent Bridge, a spell that probably cost the Headingley match and the Ashes: and, until his statistically – but tactically unimportant – burst, undistinguished bowling at the Oval. There was no case for picking him. He bristled, but he knew. The facts of form alone were enough to make his place doubtful. Would it have been wise to send him to South Africa? He himself said 'I suppose swearing has cost me at least twenty Tests – that could have been another hundred wickets – couldn't it? – and that would have given anyone a tough record chase'. After an unconvincing summer's play, and knowing he used humorously to address Australians as 'dingoes' and congratulate them on the fact that their ancestors came from the best prisons in England, the committee could well hesitate about sending him to South Africa – a gunpowder keg for the spark of political humour. So Fred was not picked.

He worked off his indignation on Gloucestershire in one of the old blasts such as he had not produced all the season. Yorkshire declared at 425 for seven at the end of the first day and next morning, on a pitch greened by a morning freshet, he burst through with four of the first five wickets – three bowled, one caught and bowled – for eight runs. When Gloucestershire followed on, he put out Young and White in his first over to tumble them down to a defeat by an innings and 294 runs.

During the winter he went on a happy tour of Jamaica with Rothmans Cavaliers. Out there he bowled with admirable vehemance in torrid heat at a time when, after a freakish sequence of accidents, he and Roy Marshall were the only bowlers on their feet. The England team in South Africa had suffered equally grievously from injuries, so that Ken Palmer, of Somerset, on a winter coaching appointment in Johannesburg, was summoned to play in the fifth Test. It was more than Fred's dignity could bear. One non-playing day he emerged from his chalet flourishing a newspaper – 'Look at this,' he said with another wave of the paper. 'Look who's bloody opening the bowling for England in the Test in South Africa – Ian Thomson and Kenny bleeding Palmer – and here am I' – he paused for effect or perhaps for the precise word – 'bowling for ... bloody cigarette coupons'. Professional pride apart, he found Jamaica amusing – and he read *Fanny Hill* with devastating conversational consequences.

He returned to a summer quite the opposite for him, to that of 1964. His Test career ended quietly but he became once more something of a triton in the smaller pool of county cricket.

In the first two of the three New Zealand Tests he took six wickets – only one of them in the first five – at an average of

39.5. Crucially, and in sad decline from his former quality, he did not once make an early penetration. When New Zealand were 28 for four in the first innings at Lord's Rumsey had taken all four while Trueman laboured without result at the other end. The simple, sorry – belated – fact was that he could no longer produce the inspired drudgery of hostile bowling on the dead batting wickets produced for Test matches. He was not chosen again; in the subsequent – South African – series of the dual-tour summer, Brian Statham who had not played since 1963, came back at the Oval when England were already one down in the rubber, to take five for 40 and two for 105 before he, too, finally retired to the milder stresses of the county game.

Trueman, fifth in the first-class table, was once more Yorkshire's most successful bowler: they won nine Championship matches in the season and he played a decisive part in seven of them. In the county's averages he was first with 115 wickets – forty-four more than anyone else – at 11.36, by almost five the best average for the county. He took nine for 48 when he and Tony Nicholson broke through to 22 for six in the innings win over Gloucestershire: thirteen for 77 against Sussex who stood at 4 for five wickets in their first innings; seven for 59 in the Roses match at Bramall Lane. There was a century against Middlesex and in August, at Taunton – an eventful place for him – he joined with Richard Hutton in a first morning sortie when, using a strong cross wind, they cut down Somerset to 19 for five, 24 for six.

Yorkshire in general viewed one-day, over-limit cricket at first-class level with a mixture of suspicion and downright distaste. In the first Gillette Cup – of 1963 – they survived one round; the next year lost their first match. Their win in 1965 is generally remembered for Geoff Boycott's record innings of 146 in the Final. Throughout the competition, however, Trueman was a match-winner: in three of the four matches he took the early wickets which are the tactical key to winning these matches – two when Leicestershire were 23 for three; four in

Somerset's 13 for five – altogether six for 15, and he was chosen as 'Man of the Match'; all three when Surrey were 27 for three in the Final. In the other game – the semi-final with Warwickshire – he (28) and Jimmy Binks (21) rebuilt the innings from 85 for six with a stand of 52: their winning margin was only 20 runs.

On the way down from greatness, this was the last year of prosperity. He could not accept that he was no longer a great bowler: and at moments he was: but they were moments. He was thirty-four years old; he had been given some long and heavy stints and now it was apparent that they were too long and too heavy. He did not believe he had had enough. He could still, when stirred to it, make good county players look like second raters but he had used up his borrowed strength. He could no longer come back after a burst – not because he did not want to, there was nothing he wanted more – but the machinery now simply took the rest it had so long been denied.

CHAPTER FOURTEEN
The Old Sweat

Fred Trueman's final coast down to retirement was made easier – indeed, almost processional – by the fact that Yorkshire were county Champions in each of his last three seasons: and, if he was no longer the main bowling force in those performances, he made important contributions – as bowler, batsman or close catcher. If he lingered a little after he ceased to be a great fast bowler, he did not do so for material reasons, but simply because he could not believe it.

He grew old relatively gracefully, though down to the end he could, and did, blast batsmen with a string of curses. Once – against the Indians of 1967 – on a Bramall Lane wicket with some life in it, he made several balls rise quickly enough to grind the knuckles of the Indian left hander, Surti who, at the fourth or fifth blow, addressed Fred in exactly the language that he – Trueman – habitually used to batsmen. Fred, horrified – for no one had dared take such a liberty before – and perhaps this was an indication of his declining speed – went in high – if not righteous – indignation to the umpire and protested that the batsman had sworn at him. With all the judicial solemnity of cricket his complaint was forwarded to Lord's. The story went round the astonished and delighted county dressing rooms with the speed of a bush fire.

In a winning side there was much generosity, and the younger players – who genuinely respected his ability – soon found that the old thunderer's bark was far worse than his bite. He had become more expansive and expensive. The lad who had horrified his seniors with the lurid ties and hectic sports coats in his early days: who, on his first visit to London, had gone to the award-winning film, *The Snake Pit* and come out complaining that 'there weren't a sodding snake in it from start to bloody finish', was now a man who wore shirts of sparkling freshness; neat and well pressed suits; highly polished shoes; and when he fancied an occasional day's shooting, he had friends who would provide it. Surprisingly, perhaps, he had a tolerance – which could almost be regarded as fondness – for young Richard Hutton, an amateur and a Cambridge Blue – by no means a certain passport to Fred's affections – and whose father he had admired but not always liked. Richard Hutton could, and did, pull his leg amiably, even affectionately and with impunity. After one of Trueman's last major successes – his six for 20 in the second innings, to bring an innings win against Leicester at Bramall Lane in his last season – he understandably relished the performance. In the pavilion after the match – Yorkshire had no fixture next day – he leant back with a pint of beer describing, with a dash of invention, the way in which he had disposed of the different batsmen. One had been yorked; another bowled by a late in-swinger; this one caught from an off-cutter; that one made to play too soon for the slower ball; yet another caught edging an out-swinger. Richard Hutton cut in – 'You must have bowled the lot, Fred – inners, outers, yorkers, slower ones – but tell me – did you ever bowl a plain straight ball?' The answer was instant – 'Aye, I did – to Peter Marner and it went straight through him like a stream of piss and flattened all three'.

After a similar triumph Hutton achieved the only known instance of reducing Trueman to speechlessness. Again there was the tapestry of every kind of variation upon the unplayable ball until Hutton asked, 'Tell me, Fred, would you say you were a modest man?'

These were working years with a decreasing number of the old withering assaults. In 1966 he was seventeenth in the national averages, fourth in Yorkshire's, where only Don Wilson, with 105, took more than his 101 wickets for the county. That was the twelfth and last time that he took a hundred wickets in a season. The next year found him far down the first class table – forty-eighth – and fifth for Yorkshire with only fifty-seven Championship wickets: in 1968, his last season, thirty-second in the main table, he was seventh in Yorkshire's when he played in twenty-three of their twenty-eight Championship matches. In the match against the 1966 West Indians he broke the middle of their innings and doggedly took more wickets – three – in their one innings than Hall or Griffith – a couple each – in the two of Yorkshire.

In the same year he produced his best performance in a Roses match – not in general a setting in which he had outstanding success – when, after Lancashire had won the toss and batted, he took four wickets for 7 runs in an opening spell of eleven overs. His final figures for the first innings were five for 18; in the second, two for 26: Yorkshire won by ten wickets. Against Derbyshire he was at his most testing: he burst through in the old manner – three of the wickets that set their first innings at 19 for four; his 43 was the highest score of the match and he took three for 15 when Derbyshire batted again: Yorkshire by ten wickets. His first innings eight for 35 by controlled seam-up effectively defeated Essex at Bradford and he rose to his final peak when the Championship was at issue.

Yorkshire had to beat Kent outright in their last match of the Championship season to win the title; and rain shortened play. Yorkshire batted first for 210: then Trueman took two crucial early wickets – of Denness and Cowdrey – to leave Kent 9 for three: mopped up the tail and finished with four for 25. After a Yorkshire collapse to 62 for seven, he made 18 out of 27 for the eighth and ninth wickets and, before the spinners took over, bowled Denness for 0. Yorkshire won by 24 runs in the extra half hour.

Early in the same season, when Yorkshire were playing for

time on the third day at Bristol, David Allen bowled the last
ball before lunch to Trueman who gave it the most terrific
belt and was caught off a skier in front of the big scoreboard –
a long carry indeed. When he came in Close remonstrated with
him, only to receive the reply 'Nay, I were only pushing it for
a single'.

It had always been Brian Close's ideal method to use Trueman in short spells though sometimes, if he pressed he could let
him go on for a few extra overs, which sometimes showed a
profit. By 1967, though, Fred was only capable of short stints
at any appreciable pace. He was, too, easily discouraged by
the kind of sluggish wicket on which, in his mighty days, he
used sometimes to startle batsmen by his fire. He could still
occasionally be encouraged into extra effort with 'Well done,
you're going well Fred – my, that was a damned quick over'.
Equally, however, he might be 'conned' out of all danger by
the batsman subtle enough to get away with 'Hard lines, Fred;
this pitch is no good to a fast bowler; why, if there was any pace
in it, you could have done me in no time.'

He made a good start to the 1967 season. A strong MCC
batting side was 23 for seven to him and Stringer: and in the
first home match, and when Close put him on as first change, he
was nettled into five for 39 against Glamorgan. Three Kent
wickets for 20: three for 25 and one for 4 when Close used
him thriftily against Worcestershire and, again first change, five
for 39 on his nostalgic annual trip to Cambridge: again, too, he
played a useful innings there. He could not sustain it; as the
season wore on, so his figures became less impressive and he was
near the bottom of the brief version of the bowling averages
published in a newspaper on the Saturday of the Gloucestershire
match at Bristol. He had no luck at all, though he constantly
found the edge of the bat against the early batsmen and, after
an unfortunate spell immediately before lunch, as he watched
yet another outside-edged stroke go through slips to the boun-

M

dary, he raised his arm in anguish with 'These bastards have nicked me out of the bloody averages.'

In May 1968, when he reported for the Warwickshire match at Middlesbrough, Brian Close told him that he had decided to leave him out for Chris Old, and make him twelfth man. That had not happened to him since he won his county cap in 1952; and he damned the decision with a fine flourish of invective before he buckled to the duties of twelfth man. It might have been kinder to have given him the match off.

There was never again quite the same zest in his bowling; he could not *prove* the great truths any more. Five for 18 at Cambridge; the first two to make Hampshire 5 for two; two for 9; two for 24, then the dropping.

After that there is a picture in the mind of Trueman taken off after two overs in the Surrey match at the Oval – he bowled only ten in the two innings – and walking away to long-leg. The great ground, which had been so full in his early days when the two counties contended for the Championship, was almost empty. Certainly there was no one within earshot of his place at long-leg and, cap at a pathetically jaunty angle, he walked over there, his shoulders rounded, as always when he was depressed, poignantly downcast as a scolded child.

His best moments thereafter were as acting captain in the absence of Close, and much of the old swagger returned when he led Yorkshire against Lawry's Australians at Sheffield. He performed his first duty satisfactorily, won the toss and gave Yorkshire first innings which Boycott, Sharpe and Padgett cautiously developed to 271 for four on the first day: thereafter, within defensive field-settings, Illingworth, with a late flourish by Trueman and Stringer, pushed up to 355 for nine before Trueman declared. So he gave himself and Hutton nearly half an hour's bowling before lunch, and reserved a modicum of shine for the start of the afternoon session. He himself opened the bowling with the most hostile field yet seen in the match. His first ball was a beamer which hummed past Lawry's nose and, in the same over Binks, standing back, was hit on the arm by another full toss. This was a fast bowler. Redpath tried to glance him, did not middle the stroke and Binks, throwing himself a long way on the leg side, took the catch. Trueman maintained the pressure regardless of runs edged through his close field and, a few moments before lunch, Walters, playing a hesitant back stroke to Richard Hutton, got an edge and Trueman, remarkably athletically for a man of thirty-seven, dived far to his right from second slip to catch him one-handed; 36 for two at lunch. Bad light and then a storm – the wicket was covered – delayed the restart but soon Trueman caught Sheahan at slip, and ran out Chappell with a fast return from extra cover. Illingworth dealt with Inverarity and Taber and Lawry who, at last erring in his selection of the leavable and the playable ball, nudged him to Trueman in the gully. Gleeson and Connolly held up Yorkshire for a little until Trueman came back himself and, with all his old killing certainty, re-moved them both. When the ninth wicket fell and the grounds-man's assistant came out to ask him which roller he wanted, he waved him imperiously away to make the enquiry of Lawry. He duly took the last wicket: had three for 32; three catches and a run out to his credit in the innings; and asked Australia, 212 behind, to follow on. They had twenty minutes of their second innings to run that evening. Trueman rolled back a year or two and began the bowling off his long run; but it was Richard Hutton who gave him, not simply a wicket, but the one wicket he wanted. An overpitched ball swung into Lawry and hit the foot of middle-and-leg. The Yorkshire players leapt high in the air and the crowd cried its sight of the triumph to come.

Next morning, Trueman, asked his forecast of the day, said that Yorkshire would win at half past three. Hutton again took an early and valuable wicket when Redpath moved across so far to an in-swinger that he was lbw when it hit him on the back of the leg. That started the main stand of the innings,

between Walters and Sheahan. Although Trueman pressed them
with close fieldsmen, they made 50 together in an hour, with an
ease and security that exhibited the truth of the wicket. It was
a humid day and Trueman, short of a bowler – Stringer, who
had damaged a groin muscle – switched the remainder rapidly
to keep them fresh. Eventually he came back himself in much
of his old pomp: first he plucked out Sheahan's middle stump:
then, with the ball he had been striving to bowl all morning, he
pitched fractionally short of a length to Walters, straight enough
to compel a stroke, made it leave the bat and Illingworth took
the catch in the gully. The rest was a matter of tidying up,
carried out mainly by Illingworth, though Trueman intervened
to remove McKenzie. The match was won; at half-past-three,
as predicted, Yorkshire beat Australia – for the first time since
1902 – by an innings and 60 runs. It was a highly efficient performance: some fine catches were held and none dropped and
Trueman had directed the entire operation with imagination
and maximum effect. He never bowled quite so fast again. He
did, though, at Scarborough in that season, run out Keith
Fletcher with a return, on the run from long-off, which amazed
not only the batsman.

Brian Statham announced that he would retire from the first-
class game at the end of the August Bank Holiday Roses
match. In two of the finest bowling spells of his career he broke
the Yorkshire first innings to 12 for five; and when Binks and
Hutton mounted a stand, came back and cut through once
more. Yorkshire out for 61 – Statham six for 34 – at the end
were happy to settle for a draw. The Lancashire crowd stood
and cheered Statham each time he came on to the field and
each time he left it. It was a majestic exit. Soon afterwards
Fred Trueman announced his retirement. In the following
season, when Yorkshire were doing poorly, he offered to return
to the team 'if required and when available'. The Yorkshire
committee, in such an exchange of courtesies as had never
before taken place between them and their erstwhile fast bowler,

acknowledged his 'fine gesture', but explained that it was the club's policy to give the younger players all possible experience. That was the end of his county cricket. He had two profitable and happy seasons of Sunday matches with the Cavaliers. In the first-class game he returned only for a single match with the International Cavaliers against the touring Barbados team and took two wickets; but he found little to fire him and, apart from occasional, one-day, non-competitive fixtures, passed out of the game he had enjoyed and coloured for twenty years.

CHAPTER FIFTEEN

The Shutter Falls

He has some rare statistics to contemplate – and he has always cherished his figures – such as taking 2,304 wickets; only fifteen other bowlers in the history of cricket – but no one of his pace – can lay claim to more. He bowled over twenty thousand overs; which is huge labour for a fast bowler. He stands above all others in taking 307 wickets in Test Matches, (and he played in only 67 so he averaged four-and-a-half wickets a match). His average – 21.57 in Tests, 18.29 in all cricket – is the more striking for the fact that he bowled so frequently to an attacking field, often without a third man or long leg, so that the ball edged through slips or the short legs usually went for four. He scored some 9,000 runs, including three centuries of which he was inordinately proud: made 438 catches, most of them at short-leg where he fielded with remarkable alertness and a balance which could justifiably be called graceful, even at intervals of bowling at top speed in exhausting conditions.

Other cricketers have ceased to play first-class cricket and continued smoothly in or near it in the leagues, as coaches, or umpires. Fred Trueman could not do that because he was never simply a cricketer; he was purely – in method, mind and heart – a fast bowler; and he could never be less than that. For that reason he could never be a fast-medium or medium-pace bowler. There is little doubt that his experience, skill and accuracy would have enabled him to play for another three or four seasons as a capable county stock bowler. With the years his pace did, indeed, deteriorate to fast-medium; but that was, in fact, deterioration, not a compromise nor a deliberate adjustment. He was never content to be less than the fastest bowler he could be; fast-medium was not for him a technical change, but a defeat. So when at length the fact was borne in upon him that he was no longer fast, he went away.

If he had done anything else he would have destroyed an image which, even at his wildest, he had religiously maintained. There were occasions in the later years when, not as a gesture nor a threat, but from need to express the self he believed in, he dug in a bouncer which was as mild as it was predictable. It had its own particular nostalgic dignity, but a deeper pathos; for batsmen then treated it lightly who would have taken hasty evasive action in the days of his high pace.

When he ceased to be a fast bowler a life ended. No doubt there was, is, and will be a life of a person by the name of Frederick Sewards Trueman who is not a fast bowler; but that is a separate man, almost a stranger to Fred the fast bowler. This other man will not roll truculently up from short-leg, cap crumpled on head, to snatch a thrown cricket ball out of the air. He will not, having now caught his audience, set off, shoulders and arms heavy with threat, thick legs unhurriedly purposeful, to a distant mark. He will not, ringed by a tensely silent crowd, come rocking aggressively in to bowl faster – in his faith – than anyone else in the world. He will not make a threateningly propelled cricket ball cut curves in the air and angles from the pitch almost as sharp as those of his reminiscence. He will not blast out the finest batsmen of his time to a figure beyond all others. He will not lard the earth with his sweat, nor curse flukers and edgers with lurid oaths, nor damn authority. He will not shock the cricket world into half-delighted, half-awed repetition of his ribaldry. Fred did that: Fred, the fast bowler who is now cricket history – a complete chapter of it.

Asked if he had a title to suggest for this book, he rolled it off the tongue, pat as if rehearsed – 'T' Definitive Volume of t'Finest Bloody Fast Bowler that Ever Drew Breath' – and where is the batsman who would have dared to challenge that description when Fred was in his pomp?

Appendix

F. S. TRUEMAN

Career Statistics compiled by Bill Frindall

1. All First-Class Matches

BOWLING SUMMARY

Season	Overs	Maidens	Runs	Wkts.	Avge.	5 wkts. Inns.	10 wkts. Match
1949	243.3	49	719	31	23.19	1	–
1950	290.1	43	876	31	28.25	–	–
1951	737.4	166	1852	90	20.57	6	1
1952	282.4	58	841	61	13.78	5	–
1953	447.1	77	1411	44	32.06	2	1
1953–54 (WI)	320	81	909	27	33.66	1	–
1954	808.2	188	2085	134	15.55	10	–
1955	996.5	214	2454	153	16.03	8	3
1956	588.4	133	1383	59	23.44	2	–
1956–57 (I)	61	9	204	8	25.50	–	–
1957	842	184	2303	135	17.05	9	2
1958	637.5	176	1414	106	13.33	6	–
1958–59 (A)	265.1*	30	823	37	22.24	2	–
(NZ)	100.2	31	244	20	12.20	2	1
1959	1072.4	269	2730	140	19.50	6	–
1959–60 (WI)	342.3	86	883	37	23.86	2	–
1960	1068.4	275	2447	175	13.98	12	4
1960–61 (SA)	114.4	16	326	22	14.81	1	–
1961	1180.1	302	3000	155	19.35	11	4
1962	1141.5	273	2717	153	17.75	5	1
1962–63 (A)	229.3*	19	773	30	25.76	1	–
(NZ)	121.2	38	247	25	9.88	3	1
1963	844.3	207	1955	129	15.15	10	5
1963–64 (WI)	49	12	124	9	13.77	–	–
1964	834.1	171	2194	100	21.94	3	–
1964–65 (WI)	79.3	18	253	11	23.00	1	–
1965	754.4	180	1811	127	14.25	10	1
1966	859.1	203	2040	111	18.37	2	1
1967	595	135	1610	75	21.46	2	–
1967–68 (I)	18	2	58	1	58.00	–	–
1968	515	116	1375	66	20.83	3	–
1969	21	1	93	2	46.50	–	–
	15,968	3,762	42,154	2,304	18.29	126	25
and	494.4*						

(* denotes 8-ball overs)

Hat-tricks (4)

Yorkshire v. Nottinghamshire at Nottingham, 1951
Yorkshire v. Nottinghamshire at Scarborough, 1955
Yorkshire v. M.C.C. at Lord's, 1958
Yorkshire v. Nottinghamshire at Bradford, 1963

Eight Wickets in an Innings (*10*)

8 – 28	Yorkshire v. Kent at Dover	1954
	(BEFORE LUNCH ON FIRST DAY)	
8 – 31	England v. India at Manchester	1952
8 – 36	Yorkshire v. Sussex at Hove	1965
8 – 37	Yorkshire v. Essex at Bradford	1966
8 – 45	M.C.C. v. Otago at Dunedin	1958–59
8 – 45	Yorkshire v. Gloucestershire at Bradford	1963
8 – 53	Yorkshire v. Nottinghamshire at Nottingham	1951
8 – 68	Yorkshire v. Nottinghamshire at Sheffield	1951
8 – 70	Yorkshire v. Minor Counties at Lord's	1949
8 – 84	Yorkshire v. Nottinghamshire at Worksop	1962

Twelve or More Wickets in a Match

14 – 123	Yorkshire v. Surrey at The Oval	1960
14 – 125	Yorkshire v. Northamptonshire at Sheffield	1960
13 – 77	Yorkshire v. Sussex at Hove	1965
13 – 79	M.C.C. v. Otago at Dunedin	1958–59
12 – 58	Yorkshire v. Leicestershire at Sheffield	1961
12 – 62	Yorkshire v. Hampshire at Portsmouth	1960
12 – 119	England v. West Indies at Birmingham	1963

How Trueman took his Wickets

Caught	1,115
Bowled	898
Lbw	274
Hit wicket	17
Total	2,304

BATTING AND FIELDING SUMMARY

Season	Matches	Inns.	N.O.	Runs	H.S.	Avge.	100s	50s	Catches
1949	8	6	2	12	10	3.00	–	–	2
1950	14	15	9	23	4*	3.83	–	–	5
1951	30	24	7	114	25	6.70	–	–	21
1952	9	4	3	40	23*	40.00	–	–	5
1953	15	16	2	131	34	9.35	–	–	15
1953–54 (WI)	8	9	3	81	20	13.50	–	–	7
1954	33	35	5	270	50*	9.00	–	1	32
1955	31	38	8	391	74	13.03	–	1	26
1956	31	30	3	358	58	13.25	–	1	21
1956–57 (I)	2	4	2	96	46*	48.00	–	–	–
1957	32	41	14	405	63	15.00	–	1	36
1958	30	35	7	453	61	16.17	–	3	22
1958–59 (A/NZ)	17	21	2	312	53	16.42	–	1	16
1959	30	40	9	602	54	19.41	–	1	24
1959–60 (WI)	10	13	2	153	37	13.90	–	–	11
1960	32	40	5	577	69	16.48	–	3	22
1960–61 (SA)	4	5	1	139	59	34.75	–	1	2
1961	34	48	6	809	80*	19.26	–	4	13
1962	33	42	4	840	63	22.10	–	1	24
1962–63 (A/NZ)	12	14	–	194	38	13.85	–	–	9
1963	27	41	6	783	104	22.37	2	2	15
1963–64 (WI)	2	2	–	28	28	14.00	–	–	2
1964	31	39	4	595	77	17.00	–	4	19
1964–65 (WI)	3	2	–	24	13	12.00	–	–	1
1965	30	39	2	636	101	17.18	1	2	17
1966	33	43	4	448	43	11.48	–	–	22
1967	31	33	5	342	34	12.21	–	–	31
1967–68 (I)	1	2	–	42	33	21.00	–	–	1
1968	29	30	5	296	45	11.84	–	–	16
1969	1	2	–	37	26	18.50	–	–	1
	603	713	120	9,231	104	15.56	3	26	438

(* denotes not out)

Hundreds

104 Yorkshire v. Northamptonshire at Northampton, 1963
100* An England XI v. Young England XI at Scarborough, 1963
101 Yorkshire v. Middlesex at Scarborough, 1965

Most runs off one over (6-ball)

26 (440666) off D. Shackleton: Yorkshire v. Hampshire at Middlesbrough, 1965. (Yorkshire were dismissed for 23 – their lowest total in any first-class match – in the second innings.)

2. Test Matches

BOWLING SUMMARY

Season	Opponents	Overs	Mdns.	Runs	Wkts.	Avge.	5 wkts. Inns.	10 wkts. Match
1952	I	119.4	25	386	29	13.31	2	–
1953	A	26.3	4	90	4	22.50	–	–
1953–54	WI	133.2	27	420	9	46.66	–	–
1955	SA	35	4	112	2	56.00	–	–
1956	A	75	13	184	9	20.44	1	–
1957	WI	173.3	34	455	22	20.68	1	–
1958	NZ	131.5	44	256	15	17.06	1	–
1958–59	A	87 *	11	276	9	30.66	–	–
	NZ	44.5	17	105	5	21.00	–	–
1959	I	177.4	53	401	24	16.70	–	–
1959–60	WI	220.3	62	549	21	26.14	1	–
1960	SA	180.3	31	508	25	20.32	1	–
1961	A	164.4	21	529	20	26.45	2	1
1962	P	164.5	37	439	22	19.95	1	–
1962–63	A	158.3*	9	521	20	26.05	1	–
	NZ	88	29	164	14	11.71	1	–
1963	WI	236.4	53	594	34	17.47	4	2
1964	A	133.3	25	399	17	23.47	1	–
1965	NZ	96.3	23	237	6	39.50	–	–

	2,202.3 and 245.3*	522	6,625	307	21.57	17	3	

(* denotes 8-ball overs)

Seven or More Wickets in an Innings

O.	M.	R.	W.		
8.4 –	2 –	31 –	8	v. India at Manchester	1952
14.3 –	2 –	44 –	7	v. West Indies at Birmingham	1963
30.2 –	9 –	75 –	7	v. New Zealand at Christchurch	1962–63

Ten or More Wickets in a Test

12 – 119 (5–75 & 7–44) v. West Indies at Birmingham 1963
11 – 88 (5–58 & 6–30) v. Australia at Leeds 1961
11 – 152 (6–100 & 5–52) v. West Indies at Lord's 1963

Balls per wicket: 49.4   Runs conceded per 100 balls: 43.6

Trueman's Record Against Each Country

Opponents	Tests	Overs	Mdns.	Runs	Wkts.	Avge.	5 wkts. Inns.	10 wkts. Match
Australia	19	399.4 and 245.3*	83	1,999	79	25.30	5	1
South Africa	6	215.3	35	620	27	22.96	1	–
West Indies	18	764	176	2,018	86	23.46	6	2
New Zealand	11	361.1	113	762	40	19.05	2	–
India	9	297.2	78	787	53	14.84	2	–
Pakistan	4	164.5	37	439	22	19.95	1	–
	67	2,202.3 and 245.3*	522	6,625	307	21.57	17	3

In England

Opponents	Tests	Overs	Mdns.	Runs	Wkts.	Avge.	5 wkts. Inns	10 wkts. Match
Australia	11	399.4	63	1,202	50	24.04	4	1
South Africa	6	215.3	35	620	27	22.96	1	–
West Indies	10	410.1	87	1,049	56	18.73	5	2
New Zealand	7	228.2	67	493	21	23.47	1	–
India	9	297.2	78	787	53	14.84	2	–
Pakistan	4	164.5	37	439	22	19.95	1	–
	47	1,715.5	367	4,590	229	20.04	14	3

Overseas

Opponents	Tests	Overs	Mdns.	Runs	Wkts.	Avge.	5 wkts. Inns	10 wkts. Match
Australia	8	245.3*	20	797	29	27.48	1	–
West Indies	8	353.5	89	969	30	32.30	1	–
New Zealand	4	132.5	46	269	19	14.15	1	–
	20	486.4 and 245.3*	155	2,035	78	26.08	3	–

(* denotes 8-ball overs)

How Trueman Took his Wickets in Tests

Caught	161
Bowled	104
Lbw	39
Hit wicket	3
	307

BATTING AND FIELDING SUMMARY

Season	Opponents	Tests	Inns.	N.O.	Runs	H.S.	Avge.	Catches
1952	I	4	2	1	17	17	17.00	1
1953	A	1	1	–	10	10	10.00	2
1953–54	WI	3	4	1	38	19	12.66	–
1955	SA	1	2	2	8	6*	–	–
1956	A	2	3	–	9	7	3.00	4
1957	WI	5	4	3	89	36*	89.00	7
1958	NZ	5	4	1	52	39*	17.33˙	6
1958–59	A	3	6	–	75	36	12.50	3
	NZ	2	2	1	42	21	42.00	4
1959	I	5	6	–	61	28	10.16	5
1959–60	WI	5	8	2	86	37	14.33	6
1960	SA	5	8	1	99	25	14.14	4
1961	A	4	6	–	60	25	10.00	2
1962	P	4	2	–	49	29	24.50	6
1962–63	A	5	7	–	142	38	20.28	7
	NZ	2	2	–	14	11	7.00	–
1963	WI	5	10	1	82	29*	9.11	3
1964	A	4	6	1	42	14	8.40	3
1965	NZ	2	2	–	6	3	3.00	1
		67	85	14	981	39*	13.81	64

(* denotes not out)

Highest score: 39* v. New Zealand at The Oval, 1958
(Scored in 25 minutes and including three sixes off A. M. Moir)